D0960800

A NEW OWNER'S
GUIDE TO
CHINCHILLAS

JG-218

Acknowledgements

Sincere thanks to Jamie Huggins of the Chin Club; Caroline Charland of the Bunny Bunch; Charles & Ingrid Larsen of ChinWorld.com; JoAnn Frey of LuvNChins; and Lani Ritchey of California Chins.

T.F.H. Publications, Inc.
One TFH Plaza
Third and Union Avenues
Neptune City, NJ 07753

This book has been published with the intent to provide accurate and authoritative information in regard to the subject matter within. While every precaution has been taken in preparation of this book, the author and publisher expressly disclaim responsibility for any errors, omissions, or adverse effects arising from the use or application of the information contained herein. The techniques and suggestions are used at the reader's discretion and are not to be considered a substitute for veterinary care. If you suspect a medical problem, consult your veterinarian.

ISBN 0-7938-2843-0

www.tfh.com

A New Owner's
Guide to
CHINCHILLAS

Audrey Pavia

Contents

2003 Edition

Chinchillas get along well together and
can be housed in the same cage.

Do all you can to give your chin the best care possible.

Give your chinchilla time out of his cage to exercise and play.

Chinchillas are friendly, sociable pets.

Keep a firm grip on your chin when handling him.

Chinchillas make wonderful, intelligent pets.

BEFORE You Start

Chinchillas make wonderful pets for both adults and children alike. But they do require a considerable amount of care for an extended period of time, since the average chinchilla can live as long as a dog or cat. That's why you should think long and hard before bringing a chinchilla into your home. Whether the chinchilla is meant to be a pet for you or your child, you need to make absolutely certain that you are willing and able to take on the responsibility of caring for an animal.

Many people believe that chinchillas require very little care. Compared to a dog, they are relatively maintenance free. After all, you don't have to walk your chinchilla, take him to obedience school, or worry about him chasing the cat. On the other hand,

chinchillas do require a significant amount of care, as you will discover as you read through this book. Ownership of one of these unique rodents should not be taken lightly, and considerable thought should go into the decision.

Some of this soul-searching can be made easier by asking yourself the following questions:

• Are you willing to take responsibility for a chinchilla and his needs for the next 15 years or more, regardless of what life brings you?

• Do you have the time, money, and patience to take care of a chinchilla?

Your pet chinchilla will require lots of love and attention. Be sure you're ready for the commitment.

• If your chinchilla gets sick, are you willing to take him to a veterinarian?

• Will you be able to give the chinchilla enough attention and exercise?

Of course before you answer all these questions, you need to know more about chinchillas and what is involved in their care. Read through this entire book before you make your ultimate decision.

Another way to help you decide if chinchilla ownership is right for you is to offer to provide a foster home for a chinchilla (through a rescue group), or to pet-sit a chinchilla for a friend. Spending time caring for someone else's chinchilla will give you a great idea of whether or not you want to make a commitment to your own pet.

WHAT'S INVOLVED

Chinchillas are cute, easygoing pets that don't make huge demands on your attention. However, they do require daily care and exercise.

The daily chores you can expect with chinchilla ownership include feeding and changing water; removing soiled bedding and litter; and at least 2 hours of exercise or playtime outside the cage. At least once a week, you'll need to clean out the entire cage and allow your chinchilla to take a dust bath.

Other responsibilities include taking the chin to the vet should he become ill, spending extended periods of time interacting with him, and maintaining the right temperature in your home. Chinchillas cannot endure excessive heat and humidity.

THE RIGHT PET?

If you still aren't sure about whether the chinchilla is the right pet for you (versus a dog, cat, rabbit, guinea pig, or hamster), consider these unique aspects to the chinchilla:

• Chinchillas have a thick, furry coat, and fall between a rabbit and a guinea pig in size.

• Chinchillas are available in more than a dozen different colorations.

• Chinchillas are nocturnal, which means they prefer to sleep during the day and are most active in the evening and at night.

• Chinchillas are social animals but need taming and attention in order to overcome their natural shyness.

Some people are allergic to the dust that chinchillas bathe in. Make sure that you are not allergic to chinchilla dust before you bring your pet home.

• Because chinchillas are delicate animals, they should not be handled by children under the age of 10.

• Chinchillas are more vocal than rabbits, and will make squeaks, barks, and other noises.

• Chinchillas are voracious chewers, and will gnaw on just about anything.

• Chinchillas need fresh foods provided daily.

• Chinchillas need care when you are away from home. While you can leave them overnight with a supply of food and water, any longer requires help from a friend or pet sitter.

ALLERGIES

Before you go out and get a chinchilla, make sure you are not allergic to these pets. Spend some time holding chinchillas to see if you have an allergic reaction.

Many people find that while they are not allergic to the chinchilla itself, they are allergic to the dust that chinchillas must bathe in to keep their coats in good shape. If your problem is the latter, you can still own a chinchilla as long as you are careful to keep the dust away from you. You'll have to stay away from it when your chin is bathing, since the dust tends to fly everywhere, and you will probably have allergy troubles when holding your chinchilla against your body after he has bathed. Although an air-purifier can help with the situation, you will no doubt suffer from allergic symptoms if you choose to own a chinchilla.

OTHER FACTORS

If you are thinking about having a chinchilla for a pet, chances are you already have other animals in your home, too, possibly a dog or cat. Realize that if you add a chinchilla to your home, you'll have to think about how your other pets will react to this new pet—and how the chinchilla will feel about the dog or the cat.

It's important to note that in the wild, chinchillas are prey animals and hunted by other creatures. Domestic chinchillas still retain much of their wild instincts, and will probably see a dog or cat as a predator. Your chin might have good reason to feel this way if your dog or cat turns out to be aggressive toward your new pet.

Most cats don't have the urge to hunt adult chinchillas because of their larger size (large compared to a rat or mice). Dogs, on the other hand, are likely to view a chinchilla as prey, and can pose a serious danger to your chin. Part of your responsibility as a chin owner will be to keep your chin safe from your dog.

Keep in mind that ideally, chinchillas need at least a couple of hours per day of uncaged exercise. That means you'll have to provide a safe room in your home where they can run around and play. Because chins are voracious chewers, you'll have to chin-proof any room accessible to your furry pets. Consider all the factors involved before you bring a pet chinchilla into your life.

INTRODUCING the Chinchilla

While many people are just now discovering the wonders of the chinchilla, humankind has known this interesting little animal for thousands of years.

Native to South America, and specifically the foothills of the Andes Mountains of Peru, Bolivia, Chile and Argentina, the chinchilla came to the attention of the Incans early in the civilization's history. The Incans were the first to discover the chinchilla's plush fur and captured chinchillas to make coats from their fur.

When the Europeans came to South America in the 1500s, they too, discovered the chinchilla and its precious coat. Word of the chinchilla's fur spread to the Old World, and soon a demand rose for garments made from chinchilla pelts. Because these pelts were scarce, only the wealthiest of Europeans could afford the luxury of owning a coat made of this fur.

The exportation of chinchilla fur in the early 1900s nearly wiped out the wild chinchilla. Chinchillas are now extinct in their natural habitat except for central Chile, where they are considered an endangered species.

By the early 1900s, exportation of chinchilla fur had reached an all-time high. Hunters and trappers swept through the Andes searching for chinchillas for pelts. Experts believe that more then 21 million wild chinchillas were killed for their fur between 1840 and 1916. Despite the vast number of chinchillas taken, chinchilla coats remained rare and expensive. This is because it takes 140 chinchillas to make a full-length chinchilla coat.

By the 1920s, chinchillas had become virtually extinct in the wild. Individual animals were being hunted so severely they did not have time to repopulate. In 1918, the Chilean government banned the trapping of chinchillas and the exportation of their fur.

As chinchillas became more difficult to find in the wild, farmers attempted to breed the animals in captivity. They experienced little success until the 1930s, when a former mining engineer named M.F. Chapman left the Andes and returned to America with 12 chinchillas to begin a breeding program. Chapman was able to develop husbandry skills that allowed the chinchillas to thrive and reproduce. With this action, Chapman virtually began the profession of chinchilla ranching.

By the 1970s, domestic chinchilla breeding had been well established, and the chinchilla ranching industry flourished. A couple of decades later, chinchillas began to catch on as pets, where they are now kept by animal lovers primarily in Europe and North America.

While the numbers of domestic chinchillas were growing, wild populations were still declining. In 1973, the Convention on International Trade in Endangered Animals (CITES) was held among agreeing countries. A ban was enacted on the exportation and importation of live chinchillas and chinchilla pelts from South America. Today, the hunting of chinchillas is illegal, according to the Convention on International Trade of Endangered Animals (CITES).

Right now, chinchillas are extinct in their entire natural environment except one area: the Andes of central Chile. Considered an endangered species here, chinchilla populations are continuing to decline despite their protected status. Many biologists believe that diminishing habitats, caused by mining, wood collection, and livestock grazing, are the reason for the wild chinchilla's continued downfall.

Chinchillas are native to South America and the Andes Mountains of Peru, Bolivia, and Argentina.

Some organizations are working to save the chinchilla in the wild. One such group is Saving the Wild Chinchilla, Inc., a Chilean-based organization with a US chapter that works to create nature reserves in South America for wild chinchillas to live and breed.

Chins in the Wild

Understanding the behavior of wild chinchillas can be very helpful when you are interacting with your own pet chin. Domestic chinchillas still retain many of the instincts of their wild ancestors, as well as the same physical attributes.

The scientific name for the chinchilla is actually *Chinchilla*. Scientists recognize two species of chinchilla: *Chinchilla brevicaudata* and *Chinchilla lanigera*. Chinchilla species are believed to have evolved according to altitude. Chins in higher altitudes have slightly different physical characteristics than those in lower areas.

Chinchillas are members of the rodent family, so they are most closely related to mice, rats, guinea pigs, and hamsters.

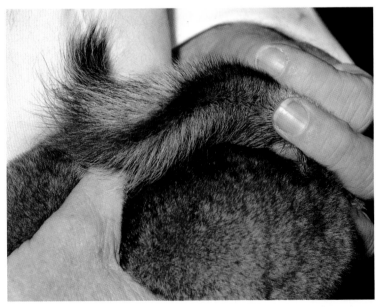

The fur on a chinchilla's tail is coarse and different in texture from the fur on the rest of the animal's body.

The standard chinchilla color is a mottled gray. Select breeding and color mutations have developed other colorations, such as beige, violet, black velvet, and white.

The average chinchilla weighs between 400 and 500 grams. About the size of a large squirrel, chinchillas have large round ears that help them stay cool in warm weather. The ears contain a series of veins close to the surface of the skin, which help cool down blood temperature.

Chinchillas also have a long bushy tail. The hair on the tail is coarse and therefore different from the fur on the rest of the chinchilla's body. The chinchilla's tail serves as a rudder when the animal is running or leaping.

Strong hind legs are another attribute of the chinchilla. Designed to help the chinchilla run, hop, and jump, these powerful back legs enable the chin to maneuver quickly to avoid predators.

Nature equipped the chinchilla with other means of self-defense. Female chinchillas that are confronted by a predator can stand on their hind legs and squirt urine directly at the attacker. All chinchillas also have anal glands that produce an unpleasant smell if they are captured or scared. This mechanism is designed to discourage predators.

Chinchillas have strong teeth designed to be able to whittle away at tough plant material and woody stems. Since grazing on such foods causes the teeth to wear down, the chinchilla is equipped with incisors that continue to grow throughout the chin's life.

Chinchillas are most well known for their plush coats, which are made up of follicles containing more than 50 hairs each (humans have one hair per follicle). The chinchilla's thick coat keeps it warm in the high altitudes of the Andes Mountains.

The standard chinchilla coat color is a mottled gray, which blends into to the animal's rocky and sandy environment in the wild. Color mutations that have been developed by breeders of domestic chinchillas are not normally seen in the wild.

In nature, chinchillas groom their coats by licking and by bathing in dust or sand. This activity is also important to the mental and physical well being of domestic chinchillas, who love to roll around in dust.

Chinchilla coats are so dense that they are not generally inhabitable to parasites like fleas, ticks, or mites. Part of the chinchilla's defense is to lose patches of fur, however, and nearly bald spots can show up on a chin's coat if the chin had a near-miss with a predator.

In nature, chinchillas live in mixed gender colonies, and make their homes primarily within the cardon plant (*Puya berteroniana*). This plant is categorized as a succulent, terrestrial bromiliad, and can be found on mountain slopes in the Andes. Chinchillas dig tunnels throughout the plant and live in the burrows they create. Some chinchilla colonies live in rocky crevices, although these chins are the exception, not the rule.

In the wild, chinchillas are weaned at about four weeks of age. Captive-bred chinchillas should remain with their mothers for about four months.

Wild chinchillas give birth to their young twice a year and usually have two babies per litter with a 111-day gestation period. The babies are born with fur and with their eyes open, and both the male and the female care for the young. By the age of four weeks, the babies are weaned from their mothers and foraging on their own.

The diet of the wild chinchilla consists of plants native to the Andean region, including rumpiato, pingo pingo, monte negro, cardon, olivillo del norte, and maravilla del campo.

You can obtain a loving chinchilla from a pet shop, a breeder, animal shelter, or a chinchilla rescue organization. Make sure the chin you take home is healthy and sociable.

Because chinchillas are nocturnal, they do most of their feeding in the early morning hours or at dusk. They are most active during this time of the day.

The chinchilla's most threatening predator is humankind, through destruction of habitat. Other predators include foxes, eagles, and hawks.

THE DOMESTIC CHINCHILLA

Chinchillas do well in captivity as long as they are properly cared for. It took chinchilla ranchers many years to discover the basics of chinchilla husbandry. As chinchillas continue to become popular pets, more is being learned about the best ways to feed and care for them.

The basics of chinchilla care include good feed with plenty of roughage, a spacious, well-constructed cage, the proper room temperature, and sufficient exercise time. Pet chinchillas provided with these elements can live long, happy lives.

Although chinchillas are kept as pets with more and more frequency, they exist in great numbers as ranch animals, bred for their pelts. Chinchilla ranchers find a good market for chinchilla pelts, with chinchilla coats selling for many thousands of dollars. Ranch chinchillas live very different lives than pet chinchillas. They are generally kept in smaller cages, and are not given the freedom to run around. They are also housed to protect their fur, and are not handled by humans for the same reason.

As the chinchilla pet market continues to grow, breeders are also producing chins bred solely as companions. These breeders usually started with one or two chins as pets and decided to get into the hobby of breeding chinchillas. Because the quality of a pet chin's coat is not as important as it is for a ranch chinchilla, pet breeders usually handle their chinchillas from a young age.

Ranchers, whose focus is to breed animals with the best fur, usually attend chinchilla shows. Pet owners are beginning to discover the fun of chinchilla shows too, although only serious pelt breeders regularly take home the big prizes. The emphasis at these shows is on chinchilla pelts, which can be disturbing to pet chinchilla owners.

On the complete opposite side of the spectrum from chinchilla ranchers are chinchilla rescue groups, private organizations made up of mostly volunteers who work to find homes for abandoned chinchillas. As a rule, these groups don't believe chinchillas should be bred for their fur, or sometimes even as pets.

WHY CHINS MAKE GREAT PETS

There is a very good reason why chinchillas are not solely used for their fur anymore. They make wonderful pets.

Ask a chinchilla owner what he or she loves about his or her chinchilla, and you'll get a long list of details. Many people love the chin for its soft, beautiful fur, available in a great number of colorations. Others find the big ears, long bushy tail, and big, round eyes to be especially charming.

For some pet owners, it's the chin's antics that top the list. Hopping across a room to see what's on the other side; spinning and twirling inside a bath house; gnawing like crazy on a wooden parrot toy—all these typically chin activities are a lot of fun to watch.

But for most pet owners, if not nearly all, the most endearing chinchilla trait is affection. Chins have an uncanny ability to make their owners feel loved. When a chin comes to greet you when you enter the room, chirping in excitement, it makes you feel wanted. When you hold your chin in your lap as you stroke his soft fur, and he looks at you with contented eyes, it's a great feeling. And when your chin sits on your shoulder as you sit at your desk or watch TV, you get the feeling there is no greater pet in the world than this.

People of all ages love to keep chins as pets. They are affectionate and charming animals.

The best way to get to know a chinchilla is to live with one. Chinchillas have a unique way of wiggling themselves into the heart of even the coolest cucumber. Care for your chin properly and give him the love he deserves, and you are bound to get volumes of love right back.

ADOPTING Your Chinchilla

Y ou've decided you want to open your home to a chinchilla or two, and are ready to start looking for your new pets. Several different options exist concerning where you can get your chinchilla. You can adopt your pet, acquire him from a breeder, or buy him at a pet store. The place where you ultimately obtain your chinchilla will depend on your personal preferences as well as what is available where you live.

Wherever you opt to acquire your pet, don't be afraid to "shop around." Look at a number of different chinchillas before you choose the one you'll take home. Remember that chins can live as long as 20 years, so the chinchilla you pick will hopefully be in your life for a long time.

RESCUED CHINCHILLAS

Rather than buying a chinchilla from a source that sells these animals, you might want to consider providing a home to a chinchilla in need. Just as with dogs and cats, homeless chinchillas are out there waiting for loving families. Usually, nothing is wrong with these chinchillas other than the fact that their owners have grown tired of them or didn't realize the responsibilities involved in chinchilla ownership.

Unlike dogs and cats, however, chinchillas aren't easy to find at a local animal shelter. Because fewer chinchillas are kept as pets, they are not seen as often in animal control facilities. However, this doesn't mean that chinchillas never become homeless. When they do, they desperately need new homes, with people who know how to care for them.

Over the past few years, chinchilla rescue groups have begun springing up around the country. People dedicated to the welfare of chinchillas make arrangements with local animal shelters to take in any chinchillas that are surrendered by owners who no longer wish to keep them as pets. These rescue groups provide food, shelter, and companionship to homeless chinchillas, and seek out new families to adopt these lovable creatures.

Rescued chinchillas come in many sizes, ages, and colorations. Often, they are perfectly friendly, well-adjusted pets that simply

In the last few years, many chinchilla rescue groups and organizations have taken in unwanted chins. Consider adopting a chin from a rescue organization and save a life.

If you adopt a baby chinchilla, be aware that chins can live for 20 years. Make sure you are able to take care of your pet for his entire lifetime.

need a new place to live. If you are considering giving a home to chinchilla, you may want to think about rescue first.

The challenge in adopting a chinchilla is finding a rescue group in your area. Since the concept of chinchilla rescue is fairly new, not all areas are serviced by these groups. If a group does exist in your area, you have several ways to try to find it.

First, try the Internet. Typing the words "chinchilla rescue" in a search engine will bring you a list of chinchilla rescue groups. You'll have to visit each website to determine where the group is located and whether it can help you.

Another option is to call your local animal shelter and ask them to refer you to a chinchilla rescue group. Veterinarians who treat exotics in your area may also be aware of chinchilla rescue groups in the community.

Try contacting rabbit rescue groups, which are in greater abundance than specifically named chinchilla rescue groups. Many rabbit rescue groups also provide rescue services to abandoned chinchillas.

If you opt to adopt a chinchilla from a rescue group, be prepared to answer questions about how you plan to care for your pet, where you will keep him, etc. Rescue groups work hard to find good homes for chinchillas and want to make sure each family that adopts a chinchilla is actually ready for one of these charming creatures.

The rescue group may also ask you to pay a small adoption fee. This is done with the purpose of weeding out unscrupulous people who may only be looking for a free chinchilla to feed to a pet reptile or for some other less than honorable purpose. Adoption fees also help chinchilla rescue groups offset the costs of caring for a homeless chinchilla until a new owner is found.

BUYING FROM A BREEDER

Another option for acquiring a chinchilla is purchasing an animal from a breeder, someone who breeds chinchillas either for show or for pets.

Pet breeders should be your first option because they are breeding chinchillas specifically with the pet owner in mind. If the breeder is responsible and caring, he or she will socialize young chinchillas from birth, and get them used to being handled. He or she will also be concerned with the chinchilla's health, and in many cases, will be willing to take the chinchilla back if you decide you cannot keep the animal.

Ask questions and check the references of a chinchilla breeder before you buy your chinchilla. A reputable breeder will be willing to answer your questions and give you a health guarantee for your new pet.

Show breeders also sell chinchillas for pets, although their primary purpose is to breed chinchillas for the coats and colors, not as pets. Show chinchillas are not handled very much since too much contact with their fur can cause it to lose the quality needed for the show pen. Consequently, these chinchillas may not be as well socialized, although adult chinchillas that have never been handled can be tamed with just a little work.

When choosing a breeder, it's important to ask some questions over the phone or via e-mail. Find out how many chinchillas the breeder has, how long he or she has been breeding, how he or she feeds the chinchillas, and how much handling they have had. Also ask if the breeder has had any health problems among the breeding animals.

A responsible breeder will welcome you, as a prospective buyer, into his or her chinchilla facility, allowing you to see the environment the chinchillas have been living in. This way, you will be able to gauge whether or not your prospective pet has been well cared for and is living in clean and healthy conditions.

Buying from a good breeder also offers an added bonus. Once you purchase your chinchilla, you'll have the name and phone number of an experienced chinchilla person who can help you with any problems that may arise.

To find chinchilla breeders in your area, try looking on the Internet first, as more and more breeders have websites to promote their breeding programs. You can also contact a local veterinarian who treats exotics. 4-H clubs

If you want a chinchilla that is a different color variety than the standard one, be prepared to pay more than for a normal chin.

Pet shops that carry chins may have a variety of colors for you to choose from. Take your time when picking out a chinchilla and make sure it appears healthy.

sometimes have chinchilla projects, and contacting your local county extension office (listed in your telephone directory) can help you find a chinchilla project leader near you.

If you want to buy from a breeder, but none can be found in your area, you may be able to find a breeder in another part of the country who would be willing to ship a chinchilla to you by air. In these situations, chinchillas fly in a carrier on a major airline in the cargo hold. The breeder will make all the arrangements for travel, and you will be responsible for paying the shipping fee.

PET SHOPS

Most people make their first acquaintance with chinchillas at pet shops. If you decide to buy your chin from a pet shop, make sure the animals are kept in a clean environment, and that they look healthy. Don't buy a chinchilla if it is housed in a crowded environment (more than one chin in a small enclosure), if the cage smells dirty, or if any of the animals seem unhealthy.

If you purchase your chinchilla from a pet shop, be sure your pet comes with a health guarantee that will allow you to return the animal if it becomes ill within a certain period of time. Take your new chin to a veterinarian right away for an examination to ensure he's healthy.

FACTORS TO CONSIDER

When looking for a chinchilla to add to the family, certain factors should be taken into consideration.

Age

Since chins live to be 15 to 20 years old, you can give a home to just about any adult chin knowing that you'll have quite a few years with that animal. If you prefer a younger chin so you will have the maximum amount of time with your pet, ask the seller or rescue group about the chin's age.

One thing you shouldn't do, however, is acquire a chin that is too young to be away from his mother. Since chins are born with all of their fur and look like miniature versions of their parents, some unscrupulous or ignorant sellers will try to sell babies that are much too young. Never buy a chinchilla under four months of age.

Keep in mind that when deciding the age of the chinchilla you hope to adopt adult chins are slightly more subdued than their younger counterparts. By comparison, adult chins do not bounce around quite as much as younger chins do.

Don't adopt a chinchilla that's too young to be taken from his mother. Although baby chins are born with their fur and are not helpless, they should be at least four months old when adopted.

Check the teeth on any chinchilla before you bring it home. The top two teeth should overlap the lower two teeth. There should be no broken or overgrown teeth.

Health

Another important factor to consider when acquiring a chinchilla is health. You need to select a chin that is healthy. Otherwise, you'll be inheriting potentially difficult and expensive medical problems.

You can determine a chinchilla's general health in a number of ways. First, check to see if the chinchilla's ears and nose are clean and free of discharge and debris. Next, look closely at the chin's fur. The fur of a healthy chin will be soft and plush. Matted down fur is a sign of trouble. Also, be sure to take a peek under the chin's tail. You are looking for signs of diarrhea. Diarrhea means the chin isn't well, and you shouldn't buy it. To make sure the chin does not have diarrhea, look under the cage to make sure that the chin's fecal pellets are round and hard.

Attitude is also important when determining the physical health of a chinchilla. Chins are normally bright-eyed, alert, and active. A sick chinchilla will be dull and listless. (The exception to this is during the middle of the day when most chins feel sleepy and lazy because of their nocturnal habits. Take the chin out of his cage and give him some time to wake up and move around. If he never comes out of his sleepy, quiet phase, he may be ill.)

Whether you are getting your pet from a rescue group, breeder, or pet shop, pay close attention to the chinchilla's surroundings. Are the cages clean and free of a strong ammonia odor? Are the chins kept in large cages? Do the other chins at the facility seem healthy? Keep in mind that if the chin you are thinking about taking is housed near a sick chin, your chin may come down with the same illness.

A very important part of your observation is looking at the chin's teeth. The chin's two top teeth should overlap the two lower teeth. Chins whose teeth do not overlap properly suffer from a condition called malocclusion. This condition is a serious problem in chins that can result in much grief to both the chinchilla and the owner.

The problem with malocclusion is that the chin's teeth won't wear down properly because of the way they are constructed, and the result is teeth that can grow out of control. These kinds of teeth need to be trimmed regularly by a veterinarian so they don't cause mouth infections and jaw problems. Without this regular clipping, the teeth can grow so long that they will curve back into the chin's mouth.

If you are buying from a breeder, take advantage of the situation to find out as much as you can about your chin's personality and health. Ask the breeder about the ancestors of the chin you are interested in, and what the chin's parents' personalities are like. Find out if the chin's parents had any health problems that could be genetic.

Return Policy

While you are discussing purchasing a chinchilla with the breeder, ask him or her about a return policy in the event the chinchilla becomes ill or you can no longer care for it. If you have other pets, you should find out if the breeder will take the chinchilla back if your other pets will not accept it into the household. This is also a distinct possibility if you are buying the chin as a cagemate for another chinchillas. Some chins don't get along with each other and you need to be able to return the new chin if he fights with the one you already have.

Temperament

When choosing your pet chinchilla, you will want to consider the animal's personality. If you give your chinchilla plenty of love and attention, he will most likely become a wonderful pet. To help ensure this happens, watch the personality of the chin you are considering. Look for an animal that seems curious and friendly.

Chins tend to be nervous by nature, and will dive for cover if they get scared. However, you want a chin that will recover quickly and poke his head out at you in curiosity. Such well-adjusted chins make the best pets.

On occasion, a chin will be very shy and want to avoid human contact at all costs. These cases usually indicate that the chin has not been handled very much and is unfamiliar with humans. With a little time and patience, often the shyest chins can learn to trust humans. Some chins will always remain fearful no matter how much you work with them, but the vast majority respond well to quiet, persistent attention.

If you see a chinchilla that races around his cage monotonously, the chin may have some mental problems. The other possibility is that the chin is bored, lonely, or hasn't been getting enough exercise. This behavior may change when the chin is placed in a good environment. However, if you opt to take home a chin like this, realize that your new pet may not recover from this behavior.

A chinchilla of either gender will make a great pet. Choose a chinchilla that is lively and alert.

Gender

Another point to consider is gender. Do you want a male or a female? This depends in some part on whether you plan to have more than one chinchilla.

Female chinchillas make good pets, although they can sometimes be territorial with other chinchillas. If you have two female chins, they may take a long time to learn to become friends. Or, they may never get used to each other. Just as with dogs, chinchillas maintain a certain pecking order in their ranks, with some individuals being more dominant than others. If you get two dominant females and try to keep them together, you'll have trouble.

Two male chinchillas, however, can get along famously. Unlike their cousin, the rabbit, male chinchillas rarely fight and seem to get along well.

Keeping a male and female together will result in baby chinchillas, and this is something all new chinchilla owners should avoid. Only knowledgeable breeders should be producing chinchillas. Also, with the growing number of abandoned chinchillas in need of homes, there is no need for pet owners to breed even more chinchillas.

To figure out if the chinchilla you are considering buying is a male or a female, you will need to examine the animal's genitalia, located under the chinchilla's tail.

The genitalia of both the male and the female chinchilla consist of a fleshy knob located near the anus. In the female chinchilla, the knob is very close to the anus, but in the male, a considerable amount of skin separates the knob and the anus. In males over the age of three months, testicles will also be present.

Whatever gender you choose, remember that the way you introduce your chins to each other can have a huge impact on how they get along together down the road.

The best combinations of gender for chinchilla cagemates seem to be two males who are father and son, or brothers. Two females who are mother and daughter or sisters can work out, as can two females who are closely related in another way. Males who are closely related can also get along, even if they are not father and son or brothers.

THE FIRST FEW DAYS

The day your new chinchilla comes into your home will be an exciting one. The entire family will be anxious to touch him and watch him explore his new surroundings.

As exciting as this will be for you, it's vital to understand that your chinchilla will probably be pretty scared by the new situation. Your chin's surroundings will be completely new to him, and he'll be surrounded by people he doesn't know. He is bound to be frightened by the entire experience.

Chinchillas have a strong instinct to avoid predators, and being in new surroundings will certainly amplify that instinct in your pet. He will be skittish and fearful at first, tending to hide and avoid

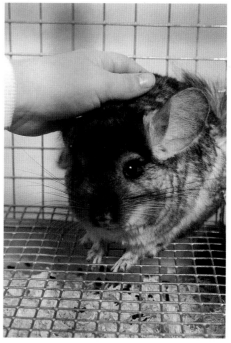

Allow your chinchilla some quiet time in his cage when you first bring him home. Let him get used to you and his new surroundings.

handling. This is normal for a chinchilla that has been moved to a new home. Remember that in time your pet will gradually become relaxed in his new environment. You can help him with this transition by giving him plenty of patience and understanding. Make sure he has a place to hide within his cage, and give him lots of "space."

The kindest way to let your chinchilla get used to his new home is to simply let him be. Equip his cage with food, water, and everything he needs, and then back off so he can get used to his surroundings.

After a day or so, your chinchilla will feel more comfortable in his cage. You can then spend time quietly observing him, sitting next to his cage, and speaking to him in a quiet voice. This will help soothe him and allow him to get used to your voice.

If you have children, now is the time to teach them how to behave around their new chinchilla. Most children are able to understand the notion of fear, and if you tell your child that the chin is feeling a little afraid in his new surroundings and needs quiet time, you'll see that your child will respond. Your child's exuberance may get the best of her at times, so it may be necessary to remind her now and then that the chin needs some time to himself so he can get used to his new home.

Most kids can't wait to show a new chinchilla to their friends, so you'll probably be asked if friends can come over. Wait a day or two after your chin has time to acclimate, and then have one or two friends visit at a time. Having a loud group of kids in the room is one way to terrify a chinchilla that is trying to get used to his new home, so it's best to keep the visitors to small numbers.

Chinchillas should never be handled by young children, and only by older kids who have been taught how to properly hold these delicate animals. Because chins are so cute and fuzzy, young children often want to squeeze them—which can be fatal to the chinchilla. Discourage holding of the animal for at least a week so the chin has time to settle down in his new environment.

Once you are certain your older child knows how to properly handle the chinchilla, always supervise him to make sure it is being done correctly. A chinchilla's bones are fragile, and dropping a squirming chinchilla to the ground could result in a broken bone.

If you have other pets, particularly dogs, keep them away from your new chinchilla at least for a while. New surroundings combined with a loud, curious dog will put the chin over the edge!

Eventually, you can introduce your other pets to your chinchilla, but for now, allow your chin to get used to his new life in as stress-free a way as possible.

HOUSING Your Chinchilla

I f you want your chinchilla to become a treasured member of your family, you should keep him indoors with the rest of your clan. Chins that live inside the house with their human companions live longer than chins kept outside, and bond more closely to their owners. They are also protected from predators and don't have to cope with bad weather.

By providing your chin with the right cage and accessories, you can easily create a home within your home for your new pet.

THE CAGE

It's a good idea to be prepared ahead of time by purchasing all the accessories your chin will need at your home. Having everything ready for your new chin when he arrives at your home will make the transition less stressful for both you and your pet.

The cage should be the first item on your list, since this is the most important object you will buy for your chinchilla. You can purchase a chinchilla cage from a pet supply store, through a catalog that sells items for small animals, or over the Internet.

When it comes to housing your chinchilla, you should buy the largest cage you can afford and accommodate in your home. In the wild, chinchillas have as much space as they need, so the more room you can give your pet chinchilla, the better.

The best cage for your chinchilla will be made of wire (aquariums are not suitable for chinchillas) and will allow at least 2 cubic feet per animal, more if you can provide it. The dimensions should be at least 12 inches wide by 16 inches high and 18 inches long. The cage should also be large enough to accommodate two shelves for the chinchilla to sit; room for a separate feeding area, bathroom area and sleeping area; room for an exercise wheel; and room for a bathing container. Keep in mind that chinchillas like tall cages and they love to climb.

Shelves for your chinchilla to perch on should be included in the cage, and should be made of hard plastic or tough, untreated pine. Chinchillas love to jump from one shelf to another, so place the shelves across from each other in the cage, and at slightly different levels.

Chinchillas have small feet and delicate legs, and so the wire mesh grid size on the sides of the cage you buy should be no more

Part of the chinchilla's cage floor can be made of wire, but be sure the chin's feet and toes cannot get stuck. A portion of the cage should have a solid floor to keep the chinchilla's feet from getting sore.

than 1 by 2 inches. Anything larger will pose a hazard to your chinchilla's safety since his legs may get caught in the wire.

A cage with a wire bottom will allow your chin's feces to drop through into a pan below. Wire bottoms shouldn't be greater than 1/2 by 1/2 inches in grid size to avoid their legs and feet getting caught. If you opt for a cage with a wire bottom, be aware that constant standing on the wire can make your chin's feet sore (a condition known as bumblefoot), so make sure the cage has a solid area where your pet can sit. This can be made from wood or hard plastic. Cages with solid bottoms are also good, although they can be harder to clean.

You can also opt to make your own chinchilla cage. If you go this route, use sturdy wire with a mesh no greater than 1 by 2 inches in grid size. Avoid using wood anywhere in the cage frame since your chinchilla will quickly gnaw it down. Study the designs of commercially made chinchilla cages to get an idea of how you should format your homemade cage. You can buy the supplies you need at a local hardware store. Don't be tempted to skimp on the quality of the materials you purchase. Your chinchilla will quickly damage a poorly made cage from cheap materials.

Buy the largest cage that you can afford, or build one yourself. If you are housing more than one chin in the cage, increase the size so each chinchilla has room to exercise and play.

CAGE ACCESSORIES

In order to be healthy and comfortable, your chinchilla needs certain accessories within his cage. You can purchase all of these items at pet supply stores that carry chinchilla products, through pet supply catalogs, or on the Internet.

Chinchillas have plenty of energy, so you'll need to provide your pet with a source of exercise within his cage. The best source of exercise is a chinchilla wheel, which is basically the chin version of a home treadmill.

When purchasing an exercise wheel for your chinchilla, be sure to choose one that is strong enough so it won't break when your chin is running full speed on it. It should also be at least 14 inches in diameter (bigger, from 15 to 18 inches is even better), and be made from a non-chewable material like metal or very hard plastic. Solid wheels are best, rather than ones made of mesh, because chinchillas can easily catch a leg or a foot in a mesh wheel. (Be sure to check the wheel every so often to make sure it's still in good condition. Wheels do wear down over time.)

You should also buy or make a hide box for your chinchilla, where he can sleep during the day and run to for security when he's

Chinchillas are active and curious animals that need toys to keep them busy. Be sure to choose ones that your chins can nibble on safely.

Chinchillas need a hide box. You can buy a plastic one in a pet store, make your own, or just give your chin a cardboard box to sleep in and nibble on.

frightened by something. If you purchase a hide box, get one made from strong, untreated wood, such as kiln-dried pine or wicker. Be aware that your chin will chew on this, and over a period of years, you may need to replace it.

You can also make a hide box from cardboard, being certain that tape and other plastics are not present on the cardboard. You don't want your chinchilla ingesting these materials when he gnaws on the cardboard—which he definitely will!

You'll need a food bowl for your chinchilla. Avoid using any old dish from the cabinet in your chinchilla cage since chins will chew up plastic, and can easily tip over any bowl not specifically designed for animal usage. Instead, you can opt for a good quality ceramic crock bowl, available at pet supply stores. Make sure the bowl is shallow enough that the chin can easily reach into it.

Another option for a chinchilla food dish is a metal or hard plastic cup that attaches to the side of your chin's cage. The benefit to this type of food dish is that your chinchilla is less likely to use it as a bathroom than he would a ceramic bowl. When selecting such a feeder, make sure it's shallow enough to allow your chin to reach all the way into it and that it is attached low enough to the side of the cage that the chin can reach it.

Fresh water is absolutely necessary for your chin's health, so it's important that you choose a good water container. The best kind of water receptacle for your chinchilla is a hanging water bottle. Known more specifically as a gravity-fed water bottle, these containers mount on the side of the cage and allow the chinchilla to drink water through the use of a metal ball in the tip of the dispenser. These bottles are readily available in pet supply stores.

A hay rack is another important item for your chinchilla's cage. Since hay is a vital element in your chinchilla's diet, hay will be a constant presence in your chin's cage. A hay rack is invaluable because it keeps the hay in one place in the cage and prevents it from being scattered around and soiled.

Most hay racks are constructed from metal and hang on the side of the cage. Your chinchilla can reach up and pull out hay whenever he feels like eating.

Other cage accessories you'll want to have on hand for your chin's arrival include chew blocks and toys. Chew blocks can be purchased from pet supply retailers that carry products for small animals. If you opt to make your own chew blocks, be sure to use

Chinchillas should have a dust bath at least three times a week. You can leave the dust bath in the chin's cage, or provide a separate place for bathing.

untreated, non-toxic wood. (Never use cedar, plum, cherry, oleander, or redwood with chinchillas, as these woods are toxic.)

Some favorite toys of chinchillas include untreated wicker baskets, wooden toys, cardboard tubes (the kind that come with rolls of toilet paper), and other assorted commercial items designed for chinchillas and rabbits.

BEDDING

To help make your chinchilla's new home as cozy as can be, you'll want to have bedding on hand when your new pet arrives.

The best bedding for chinchillas is up for debate. Bedding with strong aromas, such as cedar, is hazardous to a chinchilla's respiratory health. To be on the safe side, many chinchilla owners use kiln dried pine or recycled paper bedding. Kiln dried pine bedding is available through specialty retailers who sell small animal products, while recycled paper bedding is available at pet supply stores.

Place the bedding inside your chinchilla's hide box so he can snuggle deep inside. Don't be surprised if the bedding ends up all over the cage in due time.

Other Items

Besides the cage items listed previously, you will need a few other items for your chinchilla.

Since chinchillas need to bathe in dust at least three times a week to keep their coats healthy, you should purchase a supply of chinchilla dust powder. Your chinchilla can bathe in a homemade "bathtub," although it's wise to purchase a specially constructed bathhouse for your chin. These commercial containers do a good job of keeping the dust inside during the bath, instead of scattering it all over the place. Most are shaped like a house with a hole for the entrance, and are made of translucent plastic. The translucent plastic allows you to see inside the house and watch your chinchilla spin, roll, and do somersaults while taking a bath.

If you prefer to use a homemade bathing container, try a bowl made from ceramic or stainless steel. You can also use a large glass (large enough for your chin to squeeze into), a plastic tub (the kind you use for hand washing clothes) or a plastic gallon jug.

Chinchillas love to bathe together, so if you use a homemade bathhouse and you have more than one chinchilla, make it big enough for all the chins to fit inside at the same time.

You can purchase chinchilla dust powder and bath containers from retailers who sell chinchilla supplies. Change your chinchilla's dust about once a month to ensure that it still has the beneficial consistency your chin needs. If you only have one chinchilla, do not buy a giant bag of dust. It may take you years to use it all up.

Some people are allergic to commercial chinchilla bath. If this is the case with you, you can try using a mix of ocean sand (fine) with cornstarch. Some experts believe the sand can be dangerous to a chinchilla's health (it has been identified as a carcinogen), so consult your vet if you choose to go this route.

If you use sand, be sure it is completely dry before you offer it to your chin for bathing. You can dry it outside in the sun or in an oven. Be sure it's cool before you give it to your chinchilla.

You should consider purchasing a small travel carrier for your chinchilla. A travel carrier can come in handy if you have to confine your chin while cleaning his cage, take your chin to the vet, or transport him for any other reason. Plastic airline style carriers such as those made by Nylabone® are safest for chins, and are available at pet supply stores. Be sure to line the carrier with newspaper or bedding before placing your chin inside it.

Make sure you have a sturdy plastic travel crate or carrier for transporting your chin, such as the Nylabone® Fold-Away Pet Carrier. A chinchilla can make quick work of a cardboard carrier.

CAGE LOCATION

Now that you have your chin's cage set up with everything he needs, where should you put it? You'll need to keep several factors in mind when choosing the location for your new pet's cage.

Chinchillas have thick coats designed to keep them warm in frigid temperatures. Therefore, you should make sure your chin's cage is situated in a place where the temperature will not rise above 80 degrees Fahrenheit. The cage should also be kept away from heat sources like furnaces, stoves, and radiators, and should not be subjected to direct sunlight.

Although chinchillas can withstand cold weather, it's best to place the cage in an area that is free from drafts. A consistent temperature is best for chinchillas.

Chinchillas are always looking for something new to chew on, so make certain your pet's cage is placed far away from drapes, electrical wires, or any other objects a chin might want to gnaw on. Keep in mind that your chin can reach through the cage bars, so be sure objects outside the cage are far out of reach of grasping paws.

When choosing a place for your chinchilla's cage, keep in mind that chins are nocturnal, which means they are active at night. Unless you want to be kept awake by the activities of your chinchilla, avoid situating your pet's cage in your bedroom.

Be aware that your chin will gnaw on anything he can find, such as wood, curtains, and even electrical wires. Keep an eye on your chin to make sure he doesn't ingest anything harmful.

It's a good idea to place your chin's cage in an area of the house that is frequented by people, but yet isn't the noisiest room in the house. A den, living room, or family room is suitable unless lots of loud gatherings take place there. Too much noise will make your chinchilla nervous and fearful. A home office is a great place for a chin's cage, as is a dining room.

Wherever you opt to place your chin's cage, put it up against a wall or in a corner, not in the center of the room. Your chin will find more security if his cage is tucked away against a wall or furniture instead of standing free in the middle of a busy room.

Cleaning Tips

Keeping your chinchilla's cage clean is vital if you want to avoid health problems in your pet. A cage that is not cleaned regularly is a hotbed for bacteria that can grow to dangerous levels and make your chin sick.

To keep your chinchilla's cage clean and his environment healthy, you'll need to pick up after him on a daily basis. This means removing soiled bedding and replacing it with fresh bedding every day, picking up leftover food and hay, and cleaning out the food bowls and the water bottle. If your chinchilla cage has a tray underneath a wire bottom that catches waste, you should empty this every day.

Once a week, clean your pet's entire cage with a mild bleach solution (a bucket of water with a splash of bleach), and let it dry out in the sun, if you can. While you are cleaning your chin's cage, make sure he's safely tucked away in a carrier, or confined to a chinchilla-proofed room.

TRAVELING WITH YOUR CHIN

If you go on a trip, should you bring your chin with you? The answer is probably no. Chin's aren't great travelers, and their excursions should be limited to trips to the vet or moves with the family to a new house or apartment.

Chins are sensitive creatures, and feel most secure in familiar surroundings. If you do have to travel with your chin, the best way to do it is to confine your pet to a carrier. Not only is this the most comfortable way for your chin to travel, but it's also the safest.

Carriers come in a number of styles, but the best carrier for a chinchilla is one made of hard plastic, in an airline-type design. The carrier doesn't need to be too big, just large enough for your pet to

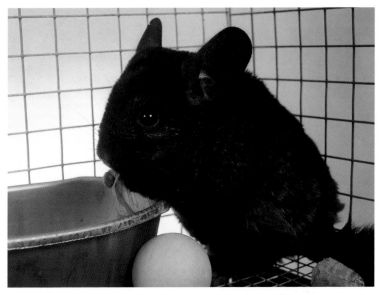

Give your chin's cage a complete cleaning once a week. It will help keep your chin healthy and happy.

If you must take your pet chinchilla outside or travel with him, make sure he can't escape. Some chins become extremely stressed when traveling and should be left home whenever possible.

turn around comfortably while sharing the space with some hay and bedding.

If you travel in the car with your chinchilla, make sure the air conditioner is on, especially if the car temperature exceeds 80 degrees. Keep your pet's carrier out of direct sunlight. If you stop for a break in your driving, resist the temptation to take your chin out of the carrier. If your pet gets loose on the road, chances are you will never see him again.

Never leave your chinchilla in a parked car during the day, even with the windows rolled down. The temperature inside the car can rise quickly, and can kill a chinchilla in a matter of minutes.

Chinchillas are good at escaping. The last thing you want is your chin to get away from you at a rest stop or another area where you won't be able to catch him. Be particularly careful about not letting your chin slip by you when you open his cage door. One way to ensure your chin's safety is to have a rule that the cage door can only be opened when the cage is inside the car, with all the doors closed and windows rolled up. That way, if your chin gets out of his cage, he will still be safely ensconced in your car.

If your road trip calls for overnight stays in a hotel, be sure to plan ahead and make reservations at hotels that allow pets. Keep your chinchilla inside his carrier when you can't supervise him while in the hotel room, and limit his out-of-the-cage exercise to the bathroom of the hotel room, since this is usually the safest place for chinchillas to roam.

Airplane rides are not recommended for chinchillas unless absolutely necessary. If you are going on a trip and must fly, leave your chinchilla in the care of a responsible friend or pet sitter. If your trip is a move to another area, then you must bring your chin on the plane with you. In this situation, plan ahead. Call the airline and make a reservation for your chinchilla in the cabin. You can put your pet's carrier under the seat in front of you if you call early enough. Most airlines allow two pets to travel in the cabin per flight.

In the event that you can't get a cabin reservation, your chin can travel in the cargo hold. Before you agree to this, make certain the airline keeps pets in a climate controlled cargo area. Cargo areas that are not climate controlled can become too hot while the plane is on the runway—a potentially deadly scenario for your chinchilla.

When you are traveling, remember to bring along everything your chinchilla will need while on the road. This includes a supply of his regular food, fresh hay, his water bottle, and fresh bedding that can replace soiled bedding when necessary.

If You Can't Take Him with You

Unless it's absolutely necessary to take your chin with you when you travel, you should leave him at home in the care of a responsible person. This could be a friend or a professional pet sitter. Another option is to board your chinchilla with your veterinarian.

If you opt to have a friend or relative take care of your chinchilla, be sure to invite that person over for a dry run before you leave on your trip. Show him or her exactly how to care for your chinchilla, including how to give your pet free time to run loose in a chin-proof room. Stress the importance of keeping your chin confined to this one room so he doesn't get into trouble elsewhere in the house.

It's a good idea to make a list of all the chores involved in caring for your chin. Don't forget to leave a number where you can be reached, as well as your veterinarian's phone number and the phone number and address of a 24-emergency vet clinic.

Hiring a professional pet sitter is a good idea if you don't have a friend or relative who is reliable and willing to care for your chin. Professional pet sitters are experienced in caring for all kinds of pets, and most also offer other services such as taking in the mail and watering plants. When interviewing the pet sitter, make sure he or she has experience in caring for chinchillas, or at least has solid knowledge of how to care for these pets.

Another option is to board your chin at your vet's office. Make sure your veterinarian has experience with boarding chinchillas before you entrust your animal to the vet and his or her staff. Find out if boarded chinchillas are kept in a room separate from boarded dogs. The last thing your chinchilla needs while you are away is exposure to barking, rambunctious canines!

NUTRITION and Feeding

I t's not hard to give your chinchilla a good diet once you know what your pet needs to stay healthy. A chin's diet is very different from that of a cat or a dog because chinchillas are rodents. They don't eat meat and are strictly vegetarian. Unfortunately, experts don't know as much about chinchilla nutrition as they do about the dietary needs of dogs and cats. Chinchilla breeders and owners often disagree about the best diet for a chinchilla, and until research is done on this topic, no one will know for certain what is the best way to feed a chin.

However, in the 50 years that chinchillas have been kept as pets in the US, breeders and owners have discovered that chins do well on a diet of chinchilla pellets, hay, and occasional treats in the form of dried or fresh fruit. The key is to always introduce new foods very gradually so as not to upset the chin's digestive system.

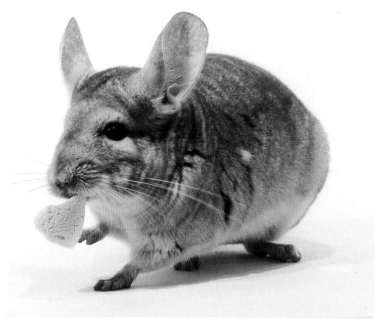

This chin is snacking on a piece of fresh fruit. Be sure to offer your chinchilla small pieces of fruit such as apples, raisins, and oranges.

PELLETS

Chinchilla pellets form the main part of a chinchilla's diet. Some people provide unlimited pellets to their chins, saying they will only eat as much as they need and will not become overweight. Others limit their chinchillas' pellets to 2 heaping tablespoons of pellets per day. This can be broken up into two feedings: once in the morning and once at night.

Chinchilla pellets typically contain alfalfa meal, soybean meal, cottonseed meal, sunflower meal, canola/rapeseed, linseed meal, peanut meal, grain by-products, and other feed ingredients. The best chinchilla pellets have a protein content of 18 percent and are low in fat.

Chinchilla pellets are designed to meet the dietary needs of chinchillas, and can be purchased from stores, catalogs, and websites that sell products for chinchillas. You should only buy as many pellets as your chin will consume in a one-month period. The longer pellets are stored, the lower their nutritional value will be.

If you are unable to find pellets formulated specifically for chinchillas (unlikely since you can order them over the Internet, at the very least), you can substitute guinea pig pellets instead.

Provide your chinchilla with a bowl of pellets and an occasional treat of fresh fruit. Your chinchilla will let you know his likes and dislikes.

Chinchillas eat with their hands, like squirrels do. Chinchilla pellets are formulated for chins and are easier to hold than rabbit or guinea pig pellets.

Substituting rabbit pellets is also an option, although only rabbit pellets made with timothy hay should be used. Remember that these feeds have not been formulated for chinchillas, and do not contain the nutrients that chinchillas specifically need. Also, chinchilla pellets are longer in shape than rabbit or guinea pig pellets since chinchillas eat with their hands, much like squirrels, and find it harder to hold onto rabbit or guinea pig pellets. Your chin would be much better off if you fed him chinchilla pellets.

Remember that if you ever need to switch your chinchilla's pellets, do so gradually. A sudden change of diet will upset a chinchilla's digestive system and give him diarrhea or sticky stools. When change is necessary, do it gradually, mixing new pellets with old pellets each day, with slightly more of the new pellets being added with time. Over a two-week period, you should have completely switched over to the new pellets.

HAY

The other very important element in a chinchilla's diet is hay. Timothy hay or bermuda hay is best (alfalfa is second best), and provides chinchillas with the large amounts of fiber they need to keep their digestive systems functioning properly.

Hay is an important part of a chinchilla's diet. It provides roughage and helps prevent hairballs.

Hay should be given in unlimited amounts and fed using a hay rack to help keep it from getting spread all over the chinchilla's cage. (This may happen even with a hay rack, but the mess might not be quite as bad.)

You can locate timothy hay at a local feed store for horses and livestock. You can also buy it packaged from stores, catalogs, and websites that sell products for small animals.

If you buy hay from a feed store, make sure it smells fresh and is free of mold before you feed it to your chinchilla.

Some people opt to give their chinchilla hay cubes instead of lose hay. The benefit of hay cubes is that they can be less expensive, easier to store, and not as messy as loose hay. The flip side is that they can be harder to find, and some chinchillas refuse to eat them. If you choose to give your chin hay cubes, try breaking them up into smaller pieces to encourage your chin to eat them.

TREATS

Chinchillas have delicate digestive systems, and too many treats can cause problems. You can give your chinchillas treats (it's especially fun to hand feed these), but you must do so in moderation so as not to upset your pet's digestive system, or cause him to get fat.

You can give fruit as a treat, but the amounts must be very tiny. One raisin per day, three or four days a week, is allowed. (Your chin will beg you for more since raisins are the favorite treat of all

Do not give your chinchilla large pieces of fruit. If he eats too much, it can upset his stomach.

Seeds also make a good treat for your chinchilla. Offer him one nut or a sunflower seed on occasion.

chinchillas, but don't give in. The sugar content of raisins is high and too many aren't good for your pet.) Or, you can opt to give one piece of other dried fruit (without sulfite preservatives), such as banana chips, dried plums, or cranberry, or a small piece of fresh fruit, like a very small piece of apple, orange, grape, carrot, or celery. An occasional unsalted nut or raw black oil sunflower seed (the kind in wild bird seed) is also allowed, but be careful not to feed these on a consistent basis because of their high fat levels. Keep in mind that all treats should add up to less than one teaspoon per day.

Your chinchilla will also appreciate another unusual treat: dried and aged twigs from an unsprayed fruit tree. Chinchillas love to gnaw on these branches and sometimes rip off the bark and eat it. Remember that it's important to dry and age the branches first since some tree branches can be poisonous if they are fresh.

OTHER NUTRIENTS

Some owners and breeders of chinchillas provide their pets with salt licks, which are round "wheels" of compressed salt and minerals. While some breeders feel this salt supplement is necessary, others do not. Those who don't provide this for their chins believe that the chinchilla pellets their pets are eating supply all the salt and minerals a chinchilla needs. Whether you opt to provide a salt lick to your

Chinchillas enjoy gnawing on dried twigs. Be sure that the twigs are free from pesticides and have been thoroughly dried.

Commercially made chew sticks make a great toy and help wear down your chin's teeth.

chin is a manner of personal choice. It certainly can't hurt your pet to have access to one of these items in his cage.

When it comes to vitamins, chinchillas that are being fed a fresh, good quality chinchilla pellet do not need vitamins added to their diet. The exception to this would be a chinchilla that is sick or has special needs. If you think you'd like to give vitamins to your chinchilla, consult your veterinarian first. Too many vitamins can be hazardous to your pet's health.

WATER

Your chinchilla cannot survive without water, and this vital part of his diet should always be available.

Your chinchilla's water should be changed daily so it is fresh. His water bottle should also be cleaned every day to prevent a build up of algae and bacteria.

Always keep an eye on the water level in your chin's water bottle. While chinchillas don't typically drink a lot of water, they should always have an ample supply in their cage.

HANDLING and Training Your Chinchilla

For many years, people didn't realize that chinchillas could make wonderful pets. Over the past several decades animal lovers have discovered that chinchillas are not only cute and fuzzy, but they are affectionate, intelligent, and a whole lot of fun. The first thing to remember when dealing with chinchillas is that although they are social creatures and love to interact with humans, they are also prey animals in the wild and have strong instincts for self protection. The result is that they can be flighty, high strung, and quick to retreat.

It's important to remember all this whenever you are interacting with your chinchilla. The slightest wrong move can send your chinchilla scurrying to his hide box or running across the floor like a bolt of lightning. Moving slowly, talking softly, and handling your pet gently are necessary, especially when you are first getting to know your chin. Eventually, your pet will learn to trust you and will let down his guard. However, chins are always capable going back into flight mode, so don't be surprised if a loud noise or a sudden appearance of a stranger sends your chin into hiding.

Chinchillas are naturally flighty and have strong instincts for self protection. Your chinchilla may appear nervous when you first bring him home.

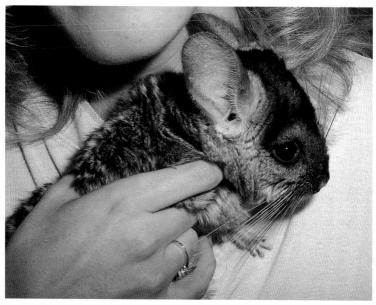

Keep a firm grip on your chinchilla when you pick him up. Hold him securely so he cannot fall and injure himself.

How to Pick Up a Chinchilla

Despite their incredibly cuddly appearance, chinchillas aren't huge fans of being held tightly. This is not to say that they don't enjoy physical contact with their humans, but they often prefer to sit on a lap or shoulder to be petted, rather than held firmly. Of course, this varies from chinchilla to chinchilla. Some are downright snuggle bugs, while others would rather not be touched at all.

Regardless of your chinchilla's personality, it's vital that you learn to pick up one of these delicate animals in the proper way. (Keep in mind that until your chin is tamed and used to you, you should avoid handling him.)

First, before you even reach for your chinchilla, speak to him in a soft, soothing voice. Chinchillas respond very well to gentle human voices and are more comfortable with people who talk quietly to them.

When it's time to pick up your chinchilla, move slowly and scoop the chin up under the body with one hand, supporting the chin's hind end. Place the other hand gently on top of the chinchilla. Hold the chin firmly but not too tight, and be careful not to let him leap to the floor. If the chin begins to struggle violently, don't fight him. Put him back in his cage and try again in a few minutes after the chin has calmed down. If the problem continues, your chin may not be tame enough to tolerate handling just yet. Work on taming him first before you start handling him.

If you have to carry your chin, support him against your chest as you walk, holding him with both hands against you.

Some chinchilla breeders lift their chins by the tail, but this is never a good idea for pet owners. Chinchillas don't like this type of handling, and in the wrong hands, this method can result in injury for the chinchilla. If you ever need to hold your chin steady for an exam or other reason, you can grasp the base of his tail with the fingers of one hand while you hold down his body against a solid surface with the other hand. Save this method for times when you must restrain you chin. Never lift your chinchilla by the ears!

If your chinchilla is not tame, but you need to take him out of his cage, try putting both hands inside his cage. Place one hand on either side of him and pull the chinchilla toward your chest. Press him close to you until you can get a firm hold on him.

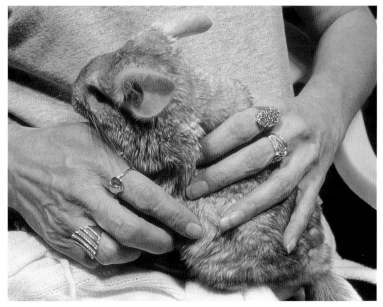

Move slowly when picking up or carrying your chinchilla. Place your chinchilla in your lap to give him a feeling of security.

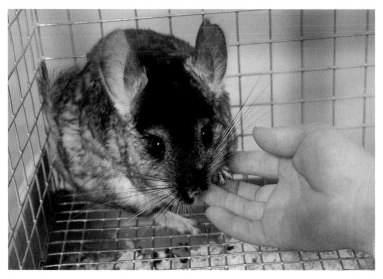

Your chin may be wary of you when you're getting to know each other. Move slowly around him and speak to him in a quiet voice to keep him calm.

Even the tamest chinchillas can be hard to catch when they are running loose in the house. The best way to capture an errant chinchilla is to corner him. Once he's in a corner, you can put your hands on either side of him and sweep him toward your chest.

If your chinchilla is hiding from you and you don't know where he is, shake his dust bath container and then leave it on the floor near you. Most likely, your chin won't be able to resist taking a dust bath, and when he enters the bathhouse, you can pick up the whole thing and place it back in the cage.

TAMING YOUR CHINCHILLA

Chinchillas are very social creatures, and so are relatively easy to tame. Even adult chinchillas that have received very little handling throughout their lives can be taught to trust and enjoy human company.

Your first step in taming your chinchilla is to let him get used to his new surroundings. Allow him a few days to get used to his new cage and the room where his cage is situated. In the meantime, you'll be reaching your hands into his cage every day to give him food and water, and to place his bathhouse inside. This will help him get used to you, as long as you move slowly and talk to him in a soothing voice while you are doing these daily chinchilla chores.

It helps to do these chores at the same time each day, preferably in the evening when your chinchilla is awake and alert. This can help establish a routine for your pet that will make him feel more secure in his new home.

Eventually, you'll notice your chin becoming more comfortable around you. Instead of diving for his hide box whenever you open the cage door, he'll stay out and watch you as you move your hands around the inside of his cage. Once this happens, you can move onto the next stage of the taming process.

Using a raisin cut in half, put your hand in your chin's cage and offer him the treat from your fingers. Once your chin starts taking the treats from you (no more than two of these treats per day so your chin doesn't get an upset stomach), you can start placing the treat on the palm of your hand. Your chin will need to crawl part way onto your hand to retrieve the goodie, and will learn to feel comfortable having physical contact with you. When your chin is touching your hand, be sure to remain perfectly still while talking to your pet in a quiet, soothing voice.

Gradually move the treat further and further up your hand, first to your wrist, then your arm. When you chin is climbing onto your arm to retrieve the treat, your pet may be ready to be held. If your chin

Try offering your chin a treat (such as a raisin) when you are hand-taming him. He will investigate the treat and soon learn to take it from your fingers.

becomes frightened and runs away from you, go back to the taming process. Your chin needs more time to get used to you.

TRAINING YOUR CHINCHILLA

You won't be able to teach your chin to Come, Sit, and Stay like you would a dog, but you can train your pet to perform some handy, rudimentary behaviors that will make living with him a whole lot easier, and more fun.

Before you can begin training your chinchilla, you need to establish a strong emotional bond between you and your pet. Your chin must trust you implicitly before you can start training him.

Some of the behaviors you can train your chinchilla to perform include coming when called, returning to cage on command, and flips or "dances." Some chins can also be taught to urinate in the same area of their cage each day.

Your primary tool when first training your chinchilla is a favorite treat. Raisins seem to work best since most chins will do just about anything for one of these treats.

In time, you can train your chin to come to you and climb on your arm. Be patient and offer him a treat as a reward for his good behavior.

Since chinchillas have a delicate digestive system that is easily upset with too many treats, you must limit the amount of treat-giving you indulge in while training your pet. For this reason, it's best to teach your chin only one of these behaviors at a time.

While you'll need treats in the very beginning to teach your chin what you want him to do, eventually, simple praise and attention will be enough reward for your pet.

Reinforcing your verbal command with a treat is one sure way to keep your chin's attention during training time.

When you first start training your chinchilla, reserve treats only for this special time of the day. Do not give out treats for "free" during the training session, but only when you are teaching a behavior to your chin.

To teach your chinchilla to come when called, pick a word, phrase or hand gesture that you want to use as a cue for your pet. It could be "Chinny, come!" or "Treat time!" or anything you desire, as long as the phrase is not too long. ("Chinny, come to Momma and get this yummy raisin!" is too long. Your chin won't be able to learn this as a verbal command.)

With the treat in your hand, approach your chin while he's in his cage or out in his exercise room and say the word or phrase you have chosen as you hold the treat out to your chinchilla. At the same time, you can use a hand signal to reinforce the verbal command. Your chinchilla will probably come to you right away to get the treat. He hasn't yet put the word or phrase and hand signal together with the treat, but if you do this twice a day for a week or so, your chin will probably catch on. Eventually, you can eliminate the treat altogether and just give him some attention as a reward or even a dust bath when he comes to you on command.

Never do anything unpleasant to your chin, like put him back in his cage right away or scold him after he comes when you call him. Doing so will teach him that coming when called means something he doesn't like, and he will soon run the opposite direction when he hears you call him.

You can teach your chin to return to his cage when you ask him to, assuming he can get to his cage on his own. You can keep the cage close to the floor so he can climb into it, or provide a ramp from the floor to the door of the cage to allow him easy access.

Teaching your chinchilla to return to his cage on command requires the use of treats. Start training this behavior by waiting until your chin's outside-the-cage playtime is over. Give the command that you plan to use ("Cage time!" for example), and take your chin back to his cage while allowing him to eat a treat as you do carry him. Do this several times, then eventually put the treat in the cage and have it waiting for him when you put him in the cage. Be sure you give the cage command beforehand. After a while, your chin will learn that every time you give the cage command, a treat can be found in his cage.

Avoid feeding your chin too many treats during training, as this can lead to obesity, upset stomach, and refusal of the regular food.

In time, you may be able to teach your chin tricks, such as flipping, or standing on his hind legs. Be sure to reward your pet when he completes the trick.

Over time, you won't have to leave a treat for him in his cage. A simple scratch behind the ears and verbal praise should suffice as reward and reinforcement.

Chinchillas can also be taught to do their special flips and dances on command. These behaviors will no doubt impress your friends. Again, you'll need your chin's favorite treat. Make sure your chin knows that you have the treat between your fingers, and then circle your hand over your pet's head as you say the words "Do flips!" or "Dance!" Your chin will follow the motion of your hand and turn his body or flip over. As soon as he performs the desired maneuver, reward him with the treat. Do this repeatedly until your chin catches on. Eventually, you can eliminate the treat and just use your hand and your voice command to get your chin to perform these tricks. Be sure to reward him afterward with plenty of love and attention.

Teaching your chinchilla to urinate in the same place every day can be useful for cage cleaning purposes. While you can't reliably teach a chinchilla to use a litter box in the way you would a cat, you may have some luck in getting him to do at least part of his business in a container that is easy to clean.

Figure out where in the cage the chin prefers to urinate. Chinchillas tend to relieve themselves in the same spot within the cage each time. Once you discover where this is, place a dish (ceramic crocks work best) filled with soiled bedding in this spot. Hopefully, your chin will catch on quickly and start using this dish exclusively for his urine.

Once he is reliably using the dish, you can switch over to cat litter (without odor control additives) or another kind of organic litter. Be sure that the litter you choose is unscented, since scented cat litter can be harmful to your chinchilla's health.

Don't get your hopes up about training your chinchilla to leave his fecal pellets in the dish. Chinchillas like to defecate whenever and wherever the mood strikes them, and can't be reliably trained to use a litter box for this purpose.

BEHAVIOR of the Chinchilla

O ne of the reasons chinchillas are becoming such popular pets is because of their endearing personalities. Chinchillas not only look cute, but they *act* adorable too. To truly appreciate your chinchilla, it helps to understand your pet's body language and vocalizations, as well as the general chin personality. If you have a thorough understanding of your chin, you will be able to bond more closely with him, take better care of him, and truly enjoy his companionship.

CHINCHILLA NATURE

In order to understand your pet chinchilla, you need to examine how his species functions in the wild. The behaviors and personality of the chinchilla is closely linked to his need for survival in the mountains, where he evolved.

In nature, chinchillas live high in the Andes Mountains of South America. They dwell in colonies made up of other chinchillas, and

Chinchillas are very social animals and get along well with each other.

create burrows in large plants growing in their habitat. Chinchillas are vegetarians, but some of the creatures they share their territory with are not. Eagles, hawks, and foxes are the chin's main predators.

In order to survive in the wild, the chinchilla has had to develop two crucial behaviors: an extreme alertness that enables it to spot predators and react quickly to them; and an ability to get along well with members of its own species. By living in groups, chinchillas increase their odds of survival and lower their risk of being eaten by a predator.

These two personality traits are very apparent even in pet chinchillas. Although your chin is now safely living in domesticity where predators are no longer an issue, he still retains those wild instincts that enabled his species to survive for thousands of years.

You can easily observe both of these traits in your pet. Your chin's alert expression and constant awareness of his surroundings should be readily apparent. Likewise, the lightning speed with which your chin moves—especially when startled—can give you a glimpse of how wild chinchillas avoid capture by predators.

Your chin's social nature should also be pretty obvious. The fact that your chin is interested in you, interacts with you, and is willing to share his space with other members of his species are dead giveaways that the chinchilla is a very social animal.

It's important to remember that chinchillas are very intelligent and have very good memories. If something unpleasant happens to a chinchilla, he will remember it for a long time.

NOCTURNAL BEHAVIOR

Unlike humans, chinchillas prefer to sleep during the day and be active at night. This goes back to the chin's wild ancestors, who felt safest from predators in the cover of night.

Dusk and dawn are the most active times for chinchillas. You will no doubt notice this preference in times of day in your pet chin. Baths, runs on the exercise wheel, and other activities will take place most often in the early morning and early evening.

For this reason, it's a good idea to schedule your feeding time, play time, and exercise time with your chinchilla at these times of the day. Your chinchilla will be most alert and active then, and will appreciate you accommodating his natural schedule.

However, this doesn't mean you can't feed or play with your chinchilla during the day. Your chin will be happy to enjoy your company during daytime hours, especially if it means treat time or time spent running loose in a chin-proofed room. Your chin may be groggy at first, but give him a few minutes to wake up. Pretty soon, he'll be wide awake, alert, and ready for action.

Vocalizations

An important way that your chinchilla communicates with you and other chinchillas is through vocalizations. Most people would assume that chinchillas are very quiet animals. They can be at times, but they also can have a lot to say when the mood strikes them.

Chinchillas have a number of vocalizations that help them communicate their feelings to those around them. Understanding the meaning of these vocalizations can help you truly understand your chinchilla.

Most chinchilla vocalizations are a variation on the chinchilla squeak. Chins have the ability to squeak both softly and loudly, at length or in short bursts, gently or with great drama. The difference in each squeak seems to be cause and intent.

Attention Squeak

One of the most adorable sounds the chinchilla makes is the squeak for attention. A soft, ongoing chortle of sorts, this vocalization is undeniably a request for interaction. If your chinchilla makes this gentle sound when you are in the room, he is probably asking you to pet him, feed him, or let him out to play.

Chins communicate with you and other chins through vocalizations. Different sounds mean different things to them, and you will soon learn what your chin is trying to tell you.

Alarm Call

Another sound used by chinchillas is the

warning alarm call. Left over from the wild, this vocalization is meant to alert other chinchillas to possible danger. The alarm call can be a sequence of loud cries, or a loud, short burst of sound. Either way, the message is clear. Something is troubling the chinchilla, and he wants everyone to know about it.

Cry of Pain or Fear

Pain is a sensation that prompts chinchillas to cry out, just as with most mammals. A shrill squeak is the chinchilla's unmistakable response to pain, and also to sudden fear. Roughly grasping a chinchilla—something you should never do—can elicit this cry, either because you have frightened the animal or because you have hurt him.

Warning Cry

Another sound that is not really a squeak, but something unique is the vocalization warning away another chinchilla or even a human, at times. A series of clicking sounds, this vocalization is a common sound that most chinchillas make from the time they are born.

Aggressive "Growl"

As cute and adorable as chinchillas can be, they can also be fighters. Known to get into it with members of their own kind, chinchillas have a distinct vocalization they use when they are fighting. A raspy snarling sound, this unmistakable noise sends a message to the other chinchilla involved in the altercation: You are toast!

Fun Antics

Chinchillas are very physical creatures, and love to move about. If you observe your chinchilla, you'll see your pet engage in a number of physical activities.

Scurrying

Let your chinchilla out of his cage for a romp, and be prepared to see a whole lot of scurrying. Your chin will be eager to investigate his surroundings, and will scurry about from one corner of the room to the other, sniffing the ground, checking out objects with his hands and teeth and generally having a good

When you let your chin out of his cage for some free time, you'll notice that he scurries around the room and investigates his surroundings.

time. If you are lucky, your chin may even scurry in your direction. Try sitting on the floor and see if he'll scurry to you, and maybe even over you!

Your chin also does a cage version of scurrying—when he gets on his exercise wheel.

Climbing

Surprisingly enough, chinchillas are enthusiastic climbers. Give them something to hoist themselves on, and they will go for it. When you turn your chin loose for his free-run time, you'll see this side of your chin's behavior in action. He'll try to climb up on whatever he can, especially if an object has areas where he can place his little hands and feet. He may even try to climb up the outside of his cage if he has access to it.

Because chins love to climb so much, it's important to limit their access to objects that are too high. If your chin falls from a high place, he could hurt himself.

Jumping

Chinchillas love to jump. If you have two shelves in your chin's cage, you've no doubt seen him jump from one shelf to another, and back and forth again. During outside play-time, your chin will find objects to jump on, across, and over.

Leaping

Chinchillas literally leap for joy when they feel like it, mostly when playing outside their cages, especially with another chinchilla. Seeing a chinchilla leap for the sheer fun of it is one of the highlights of chin ownership.

Chins like to jump and leap. Provide your chin with different levels in his cage so he can jump around and play on his own.

Hopping

You've seen kangaroos hop at the zoo and in the movies. If you are a chinchilla owner, you'll see your chinchilla do some serious hopping, too. When your chin wants to get from one side of the room to the other, and do it quickly, he'll call upon his powerful hind legs to propel him forward as he tucks his forelegs into his chest. Watching a chinchilla hop is a lot of fun, especially when you don't expect it.

Bathing

Chinchillas can be very comical creatures, especially when they are rolling and flipping. These behaviors are most commonly seen during a rite that is peculiar to the chinchilla: the dust bath.

Place a chinchilla bath house filled with chinchilla dust in front of your pet, and sit back to enjoy the fun. Your chin will enter the bath house, sniff around a bit, and then proceed to roll, spin, flip,

Chins are famous for hopping and standing on their back legs. They have a lot of energy and like to stay active.

A chinchilla is in his glory when he's bathing. Expect to see a lot of rolling, flipping, and scattering of chinchilla dust when it's bath time.

and contort himself in ways you never knew possible. Your pet will do this with lightning speed, so be careful not to blink or you might miss it!

Introducing a Cagemate

Chinchillas are very social animals, and are always happiest when they can share their lives with another chinchilla. Two chinchillas can usually co-exist happily in one cage, provided the introductions are carried out carefully, and the personalities of the cagemates are well suited.

Unlike many rabbits and guinea pigs, chinchillas can live in harmony with members of their own sex without having to be neutered or spayed. This is good news for chin owners. However, it doesn't mean that every chin will get along with every other chin. Just like humans, chins have their own personalities and simply get along better with some individuals than others.

One way to ensure that your chins will get along is to adopt two young chinchillas from the same litter. Chins that grow up together often get along best.

Another option is to introduce two chinchillas to each other when they are young. It's easier for chins to make friends with one another when they are both babies.

If you are unable to get two chins under these circumstances, or if you already have one chin and want to bring another one into the family, your next option is to try a slow and gradual introduction so the two end up liking each other in the long run.

When considering adding another chinchilla to your life, it's important to realize that it is harder to get two female chins to live together peacefully than it is to get two males to cooperate. In chinchillas, females tend to have the most dominant personalities, and two dominant females may never learn to get along.

The way you introduce your chins will have a lot of bearing on whether or not they ever grow to like each other. Chins that don't get along will fight, sometimes to the death. For this reason, it's important to follow a step-by-step procedure when introducing chins.

Your first step in chin introduction should be placing the cages of the two chins side-by-side. Don't just thrust one chin into the other chin's cage. This will result in disaster. Instead, keep their cages next to each other until you see no signs of aggression from either one of the occupants.

After a week of being peaceable next door neighbors, you can try putting one chinchilla into the other chinchilla's cage. Put the more dominant (bossiest) of the two chins in

Chins can be housed together with few or little problems. Be sure to introduce them to each other slowly. In time, they will become fast friends.

This chinchilla has made friends with a ceramic chinchilla. In time, he may get a real cagemate to socialize with.

the cage of the other chin. This will discourage the dominant chin from feeling that he has to protect his territory. Also, if you are introducing a male chin to a female chin, be sure to put the female in the male's cage, and not the other way around.

Make sure you stay in the room for most of the day to make sure the chins don't fight. If they do, you'll need to separate them and try introducing them again a few days later.

If the fighting continues when you reintroduce the two chins to each other, try switching their cages. Put one chin in the other chin's cage, and vice versa. Leave them there for a few hours. This will give each of the chins a way to get used to the other chin's scent.

Once the chins seem to be getting along okay, move both of them into a new cage with fresh bedding, food etc. The key is to have them living together in a cage that is neutral territory, free from the scent of either chinchilla.

If you find that after weeks of trying, your chins refuse to get along, don't push the situation any further. Some chinchillas can never be friends, and forcing them together could be disastrous. Chinchillas can and will fight, and are capable of inflicting terrible wounds on one another.

If your chins don't get along, keep them in separate cages and don't put them together, even during free-run time. If you had a return agreement with the breeder, pet shop, or rescue group where you adopted your new chin, you can take the chin back and try with a different one.

INTRODUCING CHINS TO OTHER PETS

Chances are, you own more pets than just a chinchilla. Many people who have chins also own dogs, cats, and parrots.

If you plan to bring a chinchilla into your home but also have a dog, cat, or parrot living with you, it's important to remember that each of your animals needs to be properly introduced to your chinchilla. This is primarily for the safety of the chinchilla, since chins are vulnerable to predatory animals like cats and dogs, and can even have trouble with aggressive parrots.

Always keep your chinchilla's safety in mind and never let your chin spend unsupervised time with another animal.

Never force pets on each other, and always supervise your animals until you are completely convinced that you can trust them alone together. Take this part of pet ownership seriously, for the welfare of your chinchilla.

Introducing Dogs

When it comes to introducing dogs to chinchillas, you have to be very vigilant about the safety of your chinchilla. Dogs are predators and can make short work of your chinchilla if you aren't careful. Most dogs have a strong chase instinct, and will catch and kill any small animal that runs from it. The exception to this is dogs that have been trained not to harm other animals. Still, even with these dogs, you can never be 100 percent certain that nothing will happen.

If you are a dog owner and want to bring a chinchilla into your life, consider the following points. Is your dog older and mellow, the type who doesn't get too excited over things? Or is she younger, active and exuberant? Older, calmer dogs are usually easier to introduce to chinchillas, whereas young, energetic dogs can pose a challenge.

Young dogs can be introduced to chinchillas, but you need to be very certain you can control your dog. Your dog must be under your complete control during the introduction process. Basically, this means your dog must have obedience training and listen to your commands without hesitation.

If your dog does not have obedience training, now might be the time to get it. A dog of any age can learn obedience, and your chin's life may depend on it. Dogs with obedience training are a joy to live with and much easier to control.

A dog with obedience training will view you as the leader of his "pack," and will take his cues from you. This is the kind of situation you want when you are introducing your dog to your chinchilla.

Let's assume your dog has been obedience trained and is controllable. How does she typically react to small animals? Does she try to chase cats and squirrels when you take her out for a walk? How does she feel when she sees a rabbit in the wild? If your dog has a strong urge to chase these creatures, you may have a problem when you try to introduce her to your chinchilla. Of course, if she is obedience trained, your dog will thwart her chasing instincts at home, if you tell her to.

If, on the other hand, you have a dog that has been encouraged to chase small animals, and has been known to catch and kill squirrels, rabbits, or other small creatures, you will be wise to keep this dog away from your chin. Once a pattern like this has been established in a dog, it is difficult to train out. Your dog will see your chinchilla as a potential prey, and you may not be able to do much to change this viewpoint.

Something else to consider is your dog's breed or mix of breeds. Certain breeds of dogs, like terriers, have been bred for hundreds of years to kill rodents. This urge is deeply inbred in them, and no amount of training is going to make them 100 percent trustworthy with a chinchilla. Other breeds of dogs, like Beagles, Foxhounds, Greyhounds, Whippets, Corgis and Siberian Huskies have also been bred to chase and kill rodents. If you have a dog of one of these breeds, or a mix of these breeds, you may find that one look at your chinchilla brings out the hunter in your canine pet. You can never completely trust a dog like this with your chinchilla.

Assuming your dog is not a hunter, and is controllable with obedience commands, you can try introducing your dog to your chinchilla through a careful, gradual process.

Before you introduce your dog to your chinchilla, make sure your chin has had time to get used to his new cage and surroundings before you bring the dog into his life. Keep the chin and the dog separated for at least several days, if not longer.

Chinchillas are fragile and may not take well to being introduced to other, larger pets such as dogs.

Once your chin seems comfortable in his new home, you can put your dog on a leash and take him into the room containing your chinchilla's cage. Make sure an adult is handling the dog, particularly one who has the dog's respect.

In the beginning, you should keep your dog away from the chinchilla's cage, and just have him sit in the same room. At the first sight of the dog, your chin will probably dive for his hide box. Eventually, he may peek out to get a look at the dog out of sheer curiosity. If he doesn't, you'll need to bring the dog into the room for a period of time every day until your chin feels safe enough to come out of his hide box at least part of the way.

Your goal here is to have the chin feel comfortable while the dog is in the room. Before you allow your dog to approach the cage, your chin should feel safe enough to come completely out of his hide box and go about his business in his cage. Keep in mind that this may take a while, but it's necessary if you are going to avoid stressing out your chinchilla.

Once your chin seems okay with your dog in the room, gradually let your dog approach the chin's cage. Once again, your chin will probably dive for cover. That's okay. Let your dog stay close to the cage, and do this daily for as long as it takes for your chin to come out of hiding.

Remember to keep your dog on his leash and quiet during this entire process. No straining, barking, or whining should be allowed, as these behaviors will scare your chinchilla.

Eventually, if your dog is well behaved, your chin will come out of his box and start going about his business. In time, he may even come over to your dog to sniff noses. Once this has happened, you know you have reached a milestone in the introduction.

In time, your dog will be able to hang out in the same room with your chinchilla while your chin is in his cage. Your two pets may even grow to like one another and find companionship together.

However, it's vital that you do not trust your dog with your chinchilla while your chin is running loose. Some dogs would never dream of hurting a chinchilla, but plenty would. Do you want to risk your chin's life by finding out which side of the fence your dog belongs?

If you have your heart set on letting your chin loose in the same room with your dog, at least muzzle your dog to make sure he can't bite your chin should he go after it. Also, try to keep such experiments limited to smaller dogs who would be less capable of doing damage to your chin. Keep in mind that even if your dog doesn't hurt your chin or even make contact with him, the reality of being chased can literally scare the life out of your chin and result in tragedy.

Introducing Cats

It's a lot easier to introduce a cat and a chinchilla than it is to introduce a chin and a dog. Most cats won't view an adult chinchilla as prey because of the chin's size. In fact, many cats tend to react with fear when they first lay eyes on a chinchilla. While we don't know for sure, we might assume that to a cat, a chinchilla looks like a giant, freakish mouse!

It's important to note that cats are predators and may be inclined to chase chinchillas that are running loose. However, cats are less capable of doing serious harm to a chinchilla than a dog. (This is not to underestimate the seriousness of cat bite on a chinchilla. Cat bites require immediate veterinary care.)

Unless you have a small space and can't adequately separate your cat and your chinchilla when your chin is in his cage or running loose, it's a good idea just to keep the cat and the chin away from each other. While some cats and chins can become fast friends, they can also become a source of anxiety for each other. The chin will most likely get the worst of this situation since cats who don't learn to ignore chins or become friends with them often want to chase them.

Your first step in introducing your cat to your chinchilla is to buy a harness for your cat and get him used to it. Your cat will wear the harness when you are introducing him to your chinchilla, thus giving you control over his behavior. In the event that your cat tries to attack your chinchilla, he won't get far if you have him on a leash and harness. You should also consider keeping a squirt gun on hand to thwart any of your cat's misbehaviors.

On the day you decide to begin your cat introductions, trim your cat's front nails. (If you have never done this before, you can have your vet show you how, or try it yourself. Simply squeeze the pad of each of your cat's front feet, and cut the tip off of each nail as it protrudes out from the paw. Don't cut too deep or you'll nip the quick and cause pain and bleeding.) If your cat's nails are clipped, he'll be less likely to hurt your chinchilla should he suddenly become aggressive.

With your cat on a harness, take him into the room where your chinchilla is safely tucked away in his cage. When your chin sees the cat, he may duck into his hide box at first, and possibly stay there for the entire session. Keep the cat in the room as long as you can, but don't allow your feline friend to approach the cage. At this point, you are just allowing the cat and the chin to get used to each other's odor and presence.

A baby chinchilla would be no match for a curious cat. Never leave your chinchilla alone with another pet, even if you think they get along together.

Eventually, your chin will peek his head out to get a look at the cat. Your cat will no doubt react to the sight of the chinchilla and will either become afraid and want to run away, or else want to approach the chinchilla to get a better look. If your cat opts to run, let him leave the room. You can't force anything on a cat, and better he be afraid of your chin than be too familiar, for the chinchilla's sake. If he wants to approach, restrain him with the leash. He shouldn't be allowed to run up to your chin's cage. The approach should be made gradually, over a period of days.

After several sessions of your cat peacefully hanging out in the same room with the chinchilla, your chin should start to feel less afraid. He will start to come out and go about his business. Some cats will do the same and just ignore the chinchilla. Others will want to stalk the chin. This latter behavior will scare the chinchilla and shouldn't be allowed. Try squirting water at your cat if he does this. If this behavior continues over a period of days, your cat may be hopeless when it comes to making friends with a chinchilla.

If your cat seems disinterested in the chin, you can eventually let the chin out of his cage with the cat present, as long as the cat is still restrained on his leash. If the cat shows no interest in chasing the chin, you can eventually allow them loose in the same room, but only with constant supervision.

Introducing Parrots

If you plan to keep a parrot and a chinchilla in the same home, you shouldn't have any problem unless your parrot is particularly aggressive and decides he doesn't like the chinchilla. If your parrot tends to get jealous if you hold another animal, or reacts aggressively when he's frightened, you may have to keep the chin and the parrot separated at all times.

You'll learn quickly if the two are going to ignore each other. Chinchillas usually have no interest in parrots, and most parrots will learn to pay little attention to a chinchilla. Just make sure you keep your chinchilla's well-being in mind whenever your parrot is in the room. A chin will run from a parrot, but a parrot may not run from a chin.

CHINCHILLAS AND DISCIPLINE

Chinchillas are generally gentle creatures and don't require much discipline. However, if you have a chin that displays occasional

If your chinchilla is nibbling on things he shouldn't, try giving him dried twigs or other objects to gnaw on. Redirect his misbehavior onto something else.

misbehaviors, you can let your pet know that you don't appreciate his antics.

Before you correct your chin, however, try to understand what is causing him to misbehave. Chinchillas don't bite very often, but when they do it's usually because they are being protective of their cage or body, are frightened, or have mistaken your finger for a piece of food.

If your chin has bitten you because you grabbed him roughly, don't correct him. You need to handle him more gently so you don't frighten him. If your chin is protective over his cage and nips you when you place your hand inside, try offering him a treat every time you reach into his cage. He'll soon come to associate your hand with something pleasant and will be less territorial when he sees it coming.

If your chin nips your finger, chances are that your finger smelled like food and your chin mistook your fingertip for a raisin. This kind of nip warrants a verbal correction on your part, to help teach your chin to distinguish between food and fingertips.

You can do this in a few ways. If your chin nips you, you can squeak very loudly, or say "Ouch!" When chinchillas bite one another, their pain and displeasure is expressed with a loud noise of protest. Your chinchilla will understand the meaning of a cry of pain.

When it comes to correcting behaviors like inappropriate chewing (on furniture, wallpaper, or books), you can correct your chin with a squirt of water from a water pistol or spray bottle. Be sure to offer your chin something that he *can* chew on after you correct him.

EXERCISE

I n the wild, chinchillas have unlimited space in which to roam. While they sleep in their dens during the day, at night, wild chinchillas run free with other members of their group, foraging for food, playing, and socializing with other chinchillas. In domestic life, chinchillas do not have this kind of freedom. Confined to cages, they depend on the kindness and responsibility of their human companions to make sure they get the workout they need, whether it's free time to roam in a safe environment, or work on the exercise wheel.

FREE-RUN TIME

One of the most challenging aspects of chinchilla ownership is finding the time and space to allow your chinchillas time to run free. Chinchillas that are always confined to a cage do not get enough exercise or mental stimulation. But chinchillas that are given hours each day to run loose provide the animal with the physical workout he needs, as well as keeping him from becoming neurotic and fearful of being outside his cage.

The amount of exercise time a chinchilla needs outside his cage each day varies, depending on which expert you ask. Some chin

Supervise your chinchilla whenever you let him out of his cage for some free time, even if he's safely playing in his dust bath.

breeders say 30 minutes a day is enough, although other experts vehemently disagree, and say the minimum amount of time any chin should be allowed to run free each day is two hours. Some experts believe that four hours a day is the optimum amount of time, and gives the chinchilla the most opportunity to exercise and explore his environment.

At first, it may sound like it's easy to give your chin this much time to run free. You just turn him loose and let him run around the house, right? Wrong! Chinchillas can get into serious trouble if they are not supervised while they are outside their cages. In order to do this right, you'll need to put your chin in a chinchilla-proofed room and keep an eye on him while he's out of his cage.

While your chinchilla is running loose in his safe environment, provide him with toys that he can play with, such as wooden blocks, cardboard rolls, boxes, untreated wicker boxes, parrot toys, cuttlebones (made for pet birds), grapevine wreaths, edible dog bones made from cornstarch, PVC pipes, empty oatmeal containers, grass mats, and anything else your chinchilla might like to play with. (Your chin will want to chew on whatever it is, so make sure it's suitable for this purpose.) You can also put your chin's bathhouse inside his playroom so he can dust himself as much as he wants during his free time.

If you have more than one chin and they all get along, let them run loose together for added fun and enjoyment. You'll not only get a kick out of watching them together, but your chins will have even more fun at playtime if a buddy is present.

CHINCHILLA-PROOFING

Before you turn your chinchilla loose for free-run time, you must chinchilla-proof the area where he will be roaming. Chinchillas are notorious for chewing on items that they shouldn't, like electrical wires, phone cords, computer cables, and antique furniture. They can also squeeze into tiny spaces and get themselves into serious trouble by getting wedged inside a fold-out couch, a reclining chair, or just about anywhere else.

For this reason, it's best to keep your chin confined to one area and not let him run around your entire living space. It's nearly impossible to make sure an entire house or apartment is completely chin safe.

Select a room for chinchilla free time that has the least amount of possible chin hazards. This should be a place where you'll have

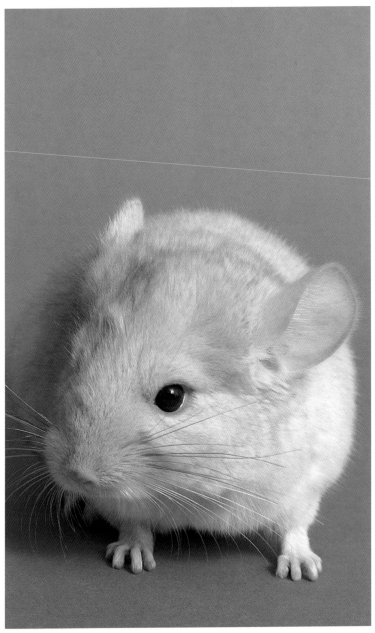

Chinchilla owners need to give their pet time out of the cage every day. You should allow your chin free time for at least 30 minutes, or longer, if possible.

Chinchilla-proof the area of your home where your chin will be allowed to roam free. Keep hazardous materials away from your chinchilla.

to do only a minimal amount of chin-proofing. Home offices are not usually a good place for chin free time because wires and cords are plentiful in these rooms. Bedrooms can be okay, as long as you don't mind having to clean chinchilla waste off your bedspread.

Many chin owners opt to use a bathroom for chinchilla free-run time. Bathrooms contain the least amount of places for chins to get into trouble. The exception to this would be bathrooms with wallpaper on the walls. Chins have been known to wreak havoc with wallpaper by chewing it up and tearing it from the walls.

Be certain that the room where your chinchilla will roam is free from any other pets that may try to chase the chinchilla. This includes dogs, cats, and parrots. If another animal starts chasing a chinchilla, it can literally scare the chin to death, or hurt the chin once the chin is caught.

Another potential hazard you should keep out of your chinchilla's reach is houseplants. Many houseplants are toxic to chinchillas, although the chins don't know that. They may decide to nibble on the plant, and the results could be disastrous.

Keeping in mind that chins are likely to chew on just about anything, be aware of any lead paint or lead pipes that might be in the room you have chosen for your chin's exercise romp. If you have lead paint on the walls, or have exposed lead pipes, it's a good idea to pick a safer environment for your pet.

Remember that rooms with drapes, fabric or leather upholstery, shoes, boxes, books, and other paper or wood-based materials are often a bad choice for a chinchilla exercise room. Chins are attracted to these kinds of materials and can make sure work of your valuables if they are left unsupervised.

If you decide to let your chin run loose in your bathroom, double check the room to be certain that there are no cubby holes or crevices where your chin can wedge himself. You may have to get down on your hands and knees to find these spots. Once you do, plug them up so your pet can't go in them. Also, be certain the bathtub is empty, since your chin could easily drown if he falls into the tub. The same goes for the sink. Be sure to keep the toilet lid closed to prevent your chin from falling in and drowning.

Make sure your chinchilla does not have access to any chemicals or other toxic products that are often kept in bathrooms. Keep all cabinets tightly shut.

Chins are curious and love to chew on everything, so it's a good idea to store away your toothbrush, toothpaste, soap, make-up,

Chinchillas like to chew on anything. Be sure to keep all pillows, blankets, and bedding out of your chin's reach if you don't want them nibbled on.

hairbrushes, hair dryers, and anything else in your bathroom that your chin might decide to nibble.

Once you have safeguarded a room, place the chin inside with a few toys and a chin buddy or two, if he has any. Check on him periodically to make sure he's okay.

When chin-proofing any room, it's important to make electrical cords inaccessible to chinchillas. If a chin chews through an electrical cord that is plugged in, he is likely to be electrocuted, and may start a fire in your home.

Put electrical cords where you are *certain* that your chin can't reach them. Better yet, cover cords with aquarium tubing cut lengthwise so the cord is protected. This works not only for electrical cords, but also for telephone and computer wires, and is a good way to protect both your chinchilla and your property.

Wherever you let your chinchilla roam, be very careful when you are walking around the room where your pet is loose. Chinchillas move with lightning speed and can quickly get underfoot. More than one beloved chinchilla has lost his life by being accidentally stepped on by his owner.

EXERCISE WHEELS

Chinchillas seem to have boundless energy, especially in the middle of the night. To help give them something to do when you are busy counting sheep, you should provide your pet with an exercise wheel.

Chinchilla exercise wheels are larger than standard mouse and hamster wheels, and are made from solid material so the chin's feet and legs can't get caught in the wire. You can purchase one at a pet supply store that sells chinchilla products, or else order one through a catalog or on the Internet.

You can leave your chinchilla's wheel in his cage 24 hours a day. Doing so will allow him to take a spin on it whenever the mood strikes him. Just be sure to inspect the wheel periodically to make sure it's in good working condition. Never rely on the exercise wheel exclusively for your pet's exercise. Your chinchilla needs free time outside his cage for optimum health.

HEALTH CARE

Chinchillas are basically healthy animals if they are kept in a clean environment, fed the right diet, and are void of stress. However, despite your best efforts, your chin may become ill and require a trip to the veterinarian. Chances are, when all is said and done, your vet bills might add up to more than you actually spent for your chinchilla, but this shouldn't stop you from dealing with your chin's illness. Your chinchilla becomes a member of the family as soon as he enters your home, and deserves the same care and attention as would any pet.

CHOOSING A VETERINARIAN

If you love your chinchilla, you will make an effort to find a good veterinarian for your pet. This means doing your homework since not all veterinarians treat chinchillas.

In the last 20 years or so, more veterinarians have become interested in treating "exotics," which are animals like birds, reptiles, rabbits, and rodents. Although research in diseases that affect these animals is sorely lagging behind research for cats and dogs, veterinarians who specialize in exotic pets are becoming more knowledgeable about caring for these creatures as a result of experience.

One of your first jobs when you get your chinchilla is to locate a good exotics vet in your area. Don't wait for your chinchilla to get sick and then search for a vet. Find a vet that you like and take your chinchilla in for an examination. Not only will this give you a chance to meet the vet and make sure you trust him or her, but it will also be a great opportunity to find out if your new pet is suffering from any ailments or problems that need immediate or ongoing care.

The best way to locate a veterinarian who treats chinchillas is to ask other chinchilla owners in your area. If you obtained your pet from a rescue group or breeder, ask for a referral to a chinchilla vet from this source. If you purchased your pet from a pet store, you can ask for a chinchilla vet referral from the pet store staff.

Your last resort is to look in your local phone directory and seek out vets who advertise that they specialize in exotics.

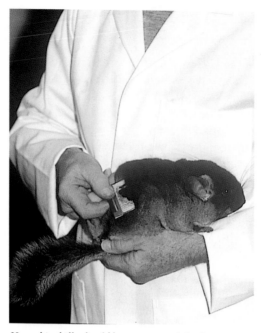

Once you have the name and number of a couple of exotics vets, call them up and ask a few questions. Find out if they treat chinchillas, and ask how long they have been caring for chinchillas. If one vet seems more knowledgeable about these animals than the others, make an appointment to bring your new chin in for a checkup.

It's a good idea to take your chinchilla in for a regular exam each year just so your vet can take a look at your

Your chinchilla should have an annual checkup to make sure that he is in the best of health.

pet and make sure all is well. At the very least, keep the veterinarian's number accessible so in the event of an urgent situation with your chinchilla, you can contact the vet quickly.

If your veterinarian does not provide 24-hour emergency services, ask for a referral to an emergency hospital that treats chinchillas, just in case you need help with your pet after-hours or on the weekends. Don't wait until an emergency strikes. Get the number now and put it in a prominent place so you will access to it when you need it.

CHINCHILLA MEDICINE

Chinchillas have not been considered popular pets in the past, and therefore not much veterinary research has been done on what ails them. Since they are considered rodents, chinchillas are assumed to suffer from many of the same problems afflicting rats, guinea pigs, and even rabbits, which are related to rodents.

Some information about chinchillas can be beneficial to know if your pet gets sick. For example, the normal body temperature for

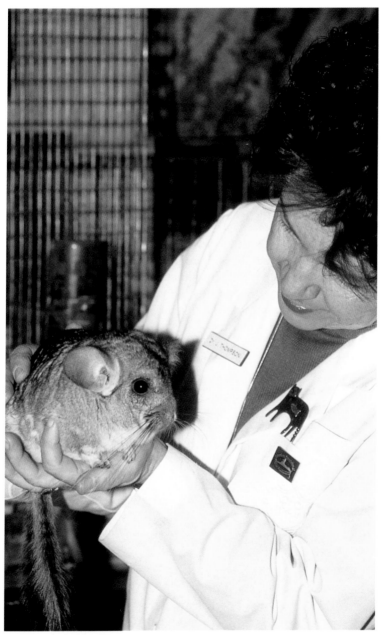

Find a vet in your area who treats chinchillas. Talk to the vet about her experience in treating "exotic" pets.

a chinchilla is 100 to 101 degrees Fahrenheit. The normal heart rate has been measured from between 100 to 159 beats per minute. Chinchillas have 20 teeth, 4 incisors and 16 molars.

Healthy chinchillas have bright, alert expressions, plenty of energy, and firm stools. The signs that your chinchilla is sick may include one or more of these symptoms: lethargy and a reluctance to move; loss of appetite; a dull expression; weight loss; discharge from the eyes or nose; diarrhea; panting or labored breathing; and seizures. If your pet shows anyone of these signs, he is in need of immediate veterinary care. Don't wait to see if your pet gets better; chinchillas can go downhill very quickly, and you may lose your chin if you hesitate to get help.

SPAY OR NEUTER?

It's always a good idea to spay or neuter any cat, dog, or rabbit you may keep as a pet. In these animals, spaying and neutering can help lengthen the pet's life by eliminating the potential for health problems related to the reproductive organs. Spaying and neutering can also eliminate unpleasant behavior problems such as aggression and inappropriate urination.

In chinchillas, however, no research has been conducted to prove that spaying and neutering prevents medical problems. Chinchillas

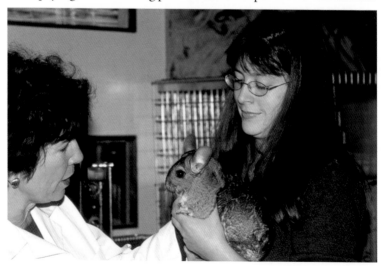

Consult a veterinarian if you have any health concerns or questions about caring for your chinchilla.

seem to get along fine with each other even when their reproductive organs are intact, leaving no reason for spaying and neutering to be performed to solve behavior problems.

Right now, the best reason to spay or neuter a chinchilla is simply to prevent the animal from reproducing. If you have a male chinchilla housed with a female chinchilla, one of these animals should be spayed or neutered to keep them from having babies.

You should not allow your chinchillas to breed. Raising young chinchillas requires considerable knowledge in chinchilla care. It also means finding responsible home for the babies, assuming they survive to adulthood. Homeless chinchillas are starting to show up in animal shelters and at rescue groups, a sure sign that there are more chinchillas out there than suitable homes for them. Under these circumstances, it's not a great idea to breed chinchillas just for the heck of it.

If you have a male and female chinchilla that you would like to house together, contact your chin vet and discuss the possibility of spaying or neutering your pet. Chances are the vet will recommend that you opt for the neuter, since this surgery is easier and less invasive than spaying.

PREVENTATIVE CARE

With chinchillas, the secret to good health is prevention. Do everything you can to keep your pet healthy. It's much easier to keep a pet in good condition than it is to try to fix a problem that resulted from improper care

The best way to keep your chinchilla healthy is to follow the advice for housing, feeding, and general care outlined in this book. In particular, make sure your chinchilla's environment is always clean. That means keeping his cage virtually spotless and washing his water bowl and food bowls every day. Change his dust bath frequently to keep it clean, too.

Use caution when introducing a new chinchilla to your existing pet. No matter how healthy your new chinchilla appears, you should quarantine him for at least a month to be sure he's healthy before you expose him to your other pet.

Feed your chinchilla the best food you can afford. Skimping on the quality of food now can result in veterinary bills later. Be sure the food you give your chin is fresh and free from mold, insects, and other contaminants. Don't be tempted to buy food in large quantities because it's cheaper. It will lose its nutritional value over time, and your chin won't be getting the nutrients he needs to stay healthy.

Give your chinchilla bottled or filtered water to be on the safe side. It can't hurt him and can possibly help him.

SIGNS OF TROUBLE

Chinchillas are usually happy, energetic creatures, but they lose energy when they are sick. If your chinchilla starts eating or drinking more or less than usual, something may be wrong. If your pet seems restless, or huddles in a crouched, listless way, take him to the vet. Also look out for a dull, itchy coat; lumps or cuts; a dirty rectal area; discharge from the nose, ears or eyes; more or less than normal urine output; a wet chin or neck; and/or strong odor from the ears or mouth.

COMMON AILMENTS

Chinchillas are prone to a number of ailments. The problems most often seen in pet chinchillas are included here.

Bite Wounds

Chinchillas are very social animals and usually live together peaceably. However, on occasion, chinchillas can fight with each other. The result is often a bite wound that, if left untreated, could become infected.

If you see what looks like a wound on your chinchilla, and the wound is not very big, you can try treating it yourself with antiseptic scrub and antibiotic ointment. Keep a close eye on the wound to make sure it doesn't become infected. (An infected wound will turn red, ooze, and refuse to heal.) If you suspect the wound is infected, contact your veterinarian immediately. The vet will likely dress the wound and prescribe antibiotics for your pet. An infected wound can be fatal to a chinchilla, so act quickly in getting veterinary care for your chin.

Constipation

Chinchillas have delicate digestive systems, and an improper diet can result in various problems. Constipation is one of these ailments.

Chinchillas suffering from constipation usually do not have enough fiber in their diets. If your chinchilla is constipated (his

Chinchillas are generally active and lively pets. If your chin stops eating or seems listless, he may be ill. Take your chinchilla to the vet at the first sign of illness.

stool is small and dry, and he seems generally uncomfortable), make certain he has access to hay at all times. Hay provides chinchillas with the roughage they need to keep their digestive systems working. Access to water is also important, since dehydration can also cause constipation.

If your chinchilla has constant access to hay and water yet still seems constipated, contact your veterinarian for help. Don't delay, since constipation can be a symptom of serious illness in chinchillas.

Diarrhea

A chinchilla suffering from diarrhea has stool that is soft and sticky, and easily flattened when you step on it. Diarrhea is a very serious problem in chinchillas, and should be treated by a veterinarian right away. Some causes of diarrhea include too many treats, bacterial infection, parasites, a change in diet, and stress.

Drooling

If your chinchilla has a constant wet area underneath his chin, he is probably drooling. Drooling is caused by problems with the teeth, most often malocclusion. Take your chinchilla to a veterinarian for an examination. If tooth problems are causing the drooling, you will need the help of your veterinarian in managing this serious problem.

Eye Problems

Because chinchillas spend time sleeping in shavings and taking dust baths, they sometimes suffer from minor eye irritations. If your chinchilla is holding his eye shut, is pawing repeatedly as his eye, and/or experiences tearing from the eye, he may have an irritation. Take him to the vet so he or she can determine the exact cause of the problem. The irritation may be caused by something as simple as a piece of dust, or can be the result of a scratch to the eye or an infection. Whatever the cause of the irritation, your vet can prescribe medication to help your chinchilla heal.

Fur Biting

The habit of fur biting in chinchillas is a lot like nail biting in humans. It is often the result of stress, and becomes a routine behavior whenever a chinchilla is exposed to a stressful environment.

You can tell your chinchilla is fur biting if you see areas on his fur that are noticeably shorter than the rest of the coat. In some

A bored, lonely, or stressed chinchilla may bite his own fur. Chewed fur will be a different color than the rest of the fur on the chin's body.

chinchilla colorations, the fur that has been chewed will be a different color than the rest of the fur in that area of the body.

Chinchillas who are bored, lonely, and/or stressed out will chew on their fur. If your chin has developed this problem, take a good look at how you are keeping your pet. Does your chinchilla get at least two hours of free run exercise time each day? If not, you need to provide at least this much time, perhaps more. Does your chinchilla have an exercise wheel in his cage? If not, installing one will help give him another way to burn off excess energy. What about toys?

Chinchillas are very social animals and they enjoy spending time with their owners. Be sure to devote time and attention to your chin every day.

If you haven't given your chinchilla toys to play with, start giving him different items to help occupy his time.

Does your chinchilla get enough interaction time with you? Chinchillas are very social animals. If your chin is alone in his cage, you need to spend time each and every day with him to make sure he's getting the kind of social interaction he needs. If you don't have enough time to do this, consider getting another chin to keep this one company.

Is your chinchilla subjected to a lot of loud noises, like screaming children, barking dogs, a washing machine, the vacuum cleaner, or other racket? Chinchillas are sensitive creatures, and frequent exposure to such noises can make your chin stressed out. Take a look at your chin's environment and remove any possible sources of stress.

Has your chinchilla undergone a recent stressful life change? Fur biting can sometimes be a reaction to losing a cagemate or moving to a new home. If this is the case, give your chin some quiet space to help him calm down. Once some time has passed and your chin has had a time to acclimate to his new life, provide him with extra toys, out-of-the-cage playtime, and more love and attention to help alleviate his stress.

Be aware that if your chinchilla is housed with another chin, it may be the cagemate that is chewing off your chinchillas fur! Try to keep an eye on the two so you can discover which one is the culprit. If you find your chin's cagemate is chewing on his buddy's fur, try giving both chins more time out of their cage. If this doesn't work, you may have to separate the two before one of your chins becomes completely bald!

Skin Fungus

Another malady that can have an affect on a chinchilla's coat is a skin fungus. Also known as ringworm, or dermatophytosis, this fungus creates bald patches on the fur and red marks on the skin. The face is a common place for this fungus to first show up on a chinchilla.

If you suspect your chinchilla is suffering from skin fungus, take your pet to a veterinarian right away. This fungus can be contagious to other chinchillas and even to humans and other pets. Your vet will diagnose the problem with a skin culture, and give you a prescription topical cream to treat the problem. You'll need to disinfect the chinchilla's cage with a dilute bleach and water solution too, to keep the fungus from coming back.

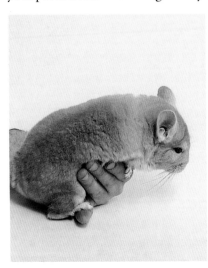

Examine your chinchilla for signs of illness whenever you handle him. He is relying on you to give him the best care possible.

Heart Problems

For reasons that aren't completely understood, chinchillas seem prone to heart problems. Enlarged hearts, blood clots in the

A chinchilla can quickly develop heatstroke if he becomes too warm. If you suspect your chin has heat stroke, cool him off and take him to the vet immediately.

heart, heart murmurs, and heart failure have all been seen in chinchillas.

You can't do much to prevent heart problems in your chinchilla other than providing him with a good diet, adequate exercise, and freedom from stress. Taking your pet for an annual exam can make it easier for your vet to detect heart problems before they become too serious.

Should your chinchilla seem under the weather—particularly if loss of appetite and lethargy are among the symptoms—don't hesitate to take your pet to a veterinarian for an exam.

Heatstroke

Chinchillas were designed by nature to live in cold climates, high in the Andes Mountains. Consequentially, their thick, dense coats do a good job of keeping the chin's body heat inside. This is great if the chin is in a cold climate. But when a chinchilla is exposed to temperatures above 80 degrees, their thick coats put them at risk for heatstroke.

Heatstroke is a very dangerous condition and is potentially fatal. When a chinchilla's body temperature goes higher than normal, damage to vital organs can result.

If your chinchilla is in a hot room or in direct sunlight and you see him panting and possibly stretched out on his side or stomach, he may be suffering from heatstroke. This is an emergency situation. Without rapid action, your chinchilla may die. Try to bring your chin's body temperature down before you take him to a veterinarian. Wrap a cold, wet towel around his body, and especially his head. If he's awake, offer him some water. If your chin is unconscious, submerge his body in cool (not ice cold) water, being careful to keep his head out of the water. Take your chin to the vet and keep a cold towel wrapped around him.

The best way to avoid heatstroke in your chinchilla is to keep him in a cool room at all times. That means leaving the air conditioner on when you aren't home if your house tends to get hot. Another way to help keep a chin cool in hot weather is to fill a large soda bottle with water, freeze it, and then keep the bottle in your chin's cage. This can do wonders to help keep your pet cool.

Your vet will do a thorough examination of your chinchilla on his first visit. The vet should check for internal parasites and other ailments.

Internal Parasites

Chinchillas are susceptible to a number of internal parasites, including giardia, coccidia cryptosporidium, tapeworm, hookworms, roundworms, and pinworms. Each of these parasites can cause serious problems with your chinchilla's digestive system.

Symptoms of these diseases include diarrhea, lack of energy, poor appearance and weight loss. (In cats and dogs, these same parasites can sometimes cause vomiting, but not in chinchillas since chins do not have the capacity to vomit.)

In most cases, only severe infestations of

tapeworm, hookworms, roundworms, and pinworms will produce these symptoms, but illnesses such as coccidia, giardia, and cryptosporidium can make your chinchilla very sick, very quickly. When you first get your chinchilla, it's a good idea to have him checked for internal parasites by your veterinarian. This involves a fecal test, where your pet's stool will be examined for signs of infection. The treatment will depend on which parasite, if any, the veterinarian finds in the exam.

Listeriosis

Chinchillas are prone to a disease called listeriosis, caused by a bacterial agent, *Listeria monocytogenes*. This bacteria attacks the chinchilla's digestive system, and causes a painful death if not treated.

Listeriosis is spread from one chinchilla to another, through contact with contaminated feces. Chinchillas have also been known to contract this disease by eating hay that has been contaminated by the feces of infected mice.

Symptoms of listeriosis include constipation, loss of appetite, and lethargy. The good news is that the bacteria can be killed with the use of antibiotics if it is caught early enough. Be sure to take your chin to the vet at any sign of illness.

Tooth Problems

A chinchilla's teeth grow throughout the animal's life. This is a handy condition in the wild since chins spend much of their awake time chewing on tough plants. In domesticity, we give our chinchillas wood and other things to chew on to help keep those teeth from getting too long.

Unfortunately, some chinchillas are born with a condition called malocclusion, where the upper and lower incisors are not properly aligned. When these chins gnaw on hard objects, their teeth do not wear down properly, causing problems for the pet.

Chinchillas can also develop other tooth problems like abscesses, loose teeth, and sharp points, often affecting the molars toward the back of the chin's mouth.

If your chin suffers from malocclusion, you will have to work to manage the condition so your pet will be able to eat properly and live a normal life. Your vet can perform certain procedures that will help your chin be able to eat normally. Your veterinarian can also treat other tooth problems.

It's important to get good veterinary care for chins with tooth problems, since the health of your chin's mouth will determine how well he is able to eat and nourish his body.

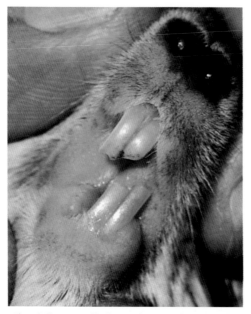

Chinchillas can suffer from a dental problem known as malocclusion. If your chin has malocclusion, his upper and lower teeth are not aligned properly and he will have trouble eating.

Respiratory Infections

Problems affecting the respiratory system are somewhat common in chinchillas, much as they are in humans. Pneumonia is one disease that is often seen in chins, along with other kinds of bacterial infections that attack the animal's airways.

Signs of respiratory distress include a runny or crusty nose, and coughing. If untreated, this can progress into lethargy and loss of appetite.

Assuming the ailment is treated early, respiratory diseases can be successfully treated with antibiotics administered by your veterinarian. Chinchillas can go downhill quickly when they are afflicted with a respiratory illness, so it's important to take your chin to the vet at the very first sign of respiratory problem.

Seizures

Chinchillas have been known to suffer from seizures. These seizures are usually a symptom of another problem, such as listeriosis, a dietary deficiency in calcium and/or thiamine, poisoning, trauma to the head, and heatstroke. Sometimes seizures are caused by epilepsy, which is a tendency to seizure due to abnormal electrical activity in the brain.

Seizures in chinchillas can differ, depending on what is causing the seizure. The chin may stiffen his body and curl himself inward, or simply lay on one side twitching uncontrollably. Staggering is another symptom of seizuring, as is a rigid posture with spasms of the feet and mouth.

If you suspect your chinchilla has had a seizure, take him to your veterinarian. Your vet can determine what caused the seizure and treat the underlying problem.

White Teeth

In chinchillas, unlike in humans, yellowish teeth are a sign of good health. Not surprisingly, white teeth in a chinchilla are a sign of a problem.

Chinchillas are born with white teeth, but as they age, their teeth turn yellow in color. White teeth in an adult chinchilla is a sign of a calcium deficiency. This problem usually only affects pregnant or nursing female chinchillas, but can show up in other chins if they are not fed a proper diet.

If your adult chin has developed white teeth, talk to your veterinarian about your pet's diet. Your vet can recommend a diet that is more sufficient in calcium than the one your chin is currently eating.

Ear Troubles

Chinchillas have big ears that can sometimes lead to trouble. Parasitic mites can take hold inside a chinchilla's ears and cause itching and irritation. Signs of mites include a dirty, waxy look inside

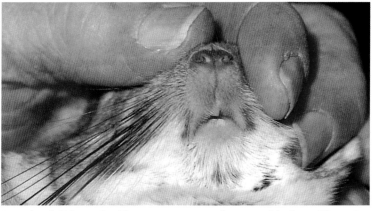

Your chinchilla's nose should not appear runny or show signs of discharge. If your chin has a runny nose, he could have a respiratory ailment. Take your chin to the vet if he begins coughing or sneezing.

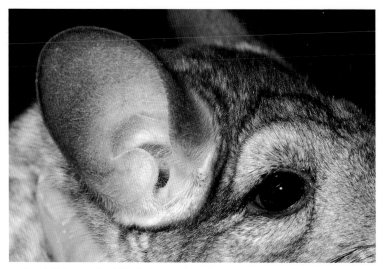

A chinchilla's ears should look clean and not have any waxy residue on the inside. If you notice your chin scratching his ears a lot, or his ears look dirty, he may have ear mites.

the ear, and frequent scratching. Your veterinarian can diagnose this problem and give you medication to put inside your chinchilla's ears.

If your chinchilla's ears get dirty, but he's not scratching at them, he probably just needs to have them cleaned. You can do this yourself with a cotton ball damped with rubbing alcohol. Clean the insides of the ears gently, without going too deep inside. Do this only when your chin's ears look particularly dirty since cleaning too often can irritate your pet's ears.

If your chin's ears become dirty quickly or have a bad odor to them, have your vet exam your chin to make sure he isn't suffering from an ear infection.

Shock

Chinchillas can suffer from shock just like humans. This is usually the result of some kind of trauma to the body, whether an injury or an illness.

The signs of shock include unconsciousness, pale mucous membranes (pale gums are most easily noted), and cold, pale paws.

If your chinchilla goes into shock, you may lose him very quickly if you don't get him to a vet immediately. Keep him warm and rush him to the hospital right away.

The After-Effects of Antibiotics

Antibiotics are valuable medications that can save your chinchilla's life if harmful bacteria have attacked his body. The flip side to this is that the antibiotics can cause digestive problems in your chinchilla. While the medication is killing the bad bacteria, it is also destroying the beneficial germs your chin needs inside his digestive system.

If your chinchilla is on a regimen of antibiotics, offer him yogurt with live culture, or a food supplement such as acidophilus. These additives to his diet can help your chin restore the good bacteria to his system.

Signs that your chinchilla is suffering from the after-effects of antibiotics including bloating, where the chin's belly swells up, diarrhea, or soft stool. Check with your veterinarian to make certain that antibiotics are causing the problem.

A chinchilla that has experienced a great deal of stress or sustained an injury or trauma can go into shock. If you think your chin is in shock, take him to the vet immediately.

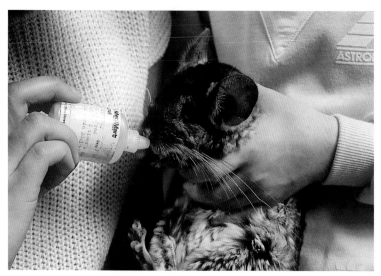

Never give your chinchilla any medications or antibiotics without your veterinarian's approval. It could do more harm than good.

CHINCHILLA FIRST AID

In case of an emergency, your first priority should be to get your chinchilla to a veterinarian immediately. However, you can take some actions to slow bleeding, etc., as you are on the way to the vet. You can also treat minor problems yourself, or check your chin's temperature to see if he is running a fever before you call your veterinarian. Knowing the chin's temperature can help your veterinarian ascertain the seriousness of your pet's situation.

Making a First-Aid Kit

Put together a chinchilla first-aid kit to use in case your chin runs into trouble and needs immediate help before he sees a vet.

Some of the items that should be included in your first-aid kit include:
- Cotton balls
- Small towel
- Antiseptic scrub
- Cotton balls
- Gauze
- Rectal thermometer
- Lubricant jelly or liquid

- Antibiotic ointment
- Styptic powder
- Scissors

You can keep all these items in a box, designated for your chinchilla. Know where it is so you can find it quickly should you need to attend to your pet in a hurry.

Dealing with Wounds

When chinchillas are kept together, they sometimes get into scuffles and bite each other. If your chinchilla has a bite that was inflicted by another chinchilla, or a wound that he obtained by hurting himself on a sharp edge or object, you can treat the injury at home as long as you keep a close watch on the wound to make sure it doesn't get infected.

Begin by using antiseptic scrub on the wound, and cleaning it with a cotton ball dampened with the antiseptic solution. If the wound is bleeding, you can sprinkle some styptic powder on it to help stop the bleeding. Next, apply antibiotic ointment to the wound. Keep an eye on it over the next few days. If it is healing well, it will scab over. If it becomes red and inflamed, the wound needs to be attended to by your vet.

Taking Your Chin's Temperature

If your chinchilla seems under the weather, you can try taking his

Would you know what do to in case of an emergency? Learn basic first aid so you can help your chin if he becomes injured.

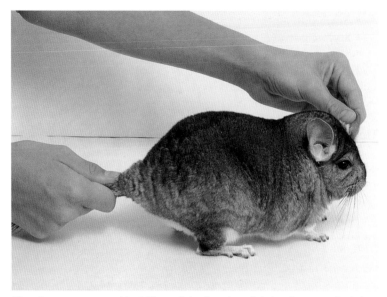

If you have two or more chinchillas and they have been fighting, be sure to check them for bite wounds or scratches.

temperature. Lubricate the tip of a rectal thermometer with lubricating jelly. Gently insert the thermometer into your chinchilla's rectum and hold it in place for three minutes. You'll need to carefully restrain your pet as you are doing this. If your chin's temperature reads higher than 101 and he is showing symptoms of illness (lethargy, loss of appetite), contact your veterinarian. If you chin's temperature is below 100 and he seems ill, call your veterinarian.

CARING FOR SENIOR CHINS

Over the last couple of decades, chinchillas have become increasingly popular as pets. Before that time, no one knew what life was like with a geriatric chinchilla.

Now that chins are being kept as pets, we are seeing how older chins are able to function in life. With life spans upwards of 20 years, it's not unusual to see senior chinchillas living as pets.

The problems experienced by senior chinchillas are typically of old age in mammals, including humans. Older chins have trouble staying warm and keeping cool. They can become slow moving and stiff at times, and don't have the same energy level as younger

Older chinchillas need special treatment and care. They may have trouble keeping warm and staying cool. Give your senior chin extra love and attention.

Be sure to provide your chin with lots of toys and other safe objects to chew on. It will help keep his teeth from becoming overgrown.

chinchillas. They don't metabolize nutrients as well as young chins do, and they sometimes have trouble with their teeth. Older chinchillas have also been known to develop cataracts in their eyes. You can tell if your chin has cataracts because you'll see a milky, opaque coloring on the surface of his eyes. Not much can be done about this problem, so it's fortunate that chins usually do a good job of adjusting to their impaired eyesight.

You can take a number of steps to help your older chin live a more comfortable life. One thing you can do is to provide more heat in cold weather than you normally would. Make certain your pet's cage is free from drafts. When the air is cold, wrap the cage in a blanket, or with cardboard (and don't be surprised if you chin chews on it).

Because older chins have trouble cooling off as well as younger chins, be sure to monitor your senior pet closely in hot weather. When the room temperature reaches 78 degrees, provide some relief for your chin, either in the form of air conditioning or by putting soda bottles filled with frozen water inside your chin's cage.

Be sure that your chin's cage is comfortable and free from sharp edges and objects where your less-dexterous pet might hurt himself. Offer him more solid area on the floor of his cage to help prevent him from getting sore feet.

Have your veterinarian check your older chin's teeth at least once a year. Senior chins sometimes have overgrown teeth that need trimming. Look at the color too. If your chin's teeth are white instead of the normal yellow, talk to your vet about what might be causing the problem.

If your senior chin starts to drop weight, it may be because he is not able to metabolize his nutrients. Take him to your vet for an evaluation. If your vet finds that your chin is healthy but simply not able to obtain as many calories from his food as he did during his younger years, he or she will give you some advice about how to feed your chin to help him put on some weight.

Older chinchillas are often plagued by certain life-threatening health problems, including kidney failure and cancer. Other age related problems that may affect your pet are arthritis, and ruptured disks in the spine. If your chin is diagnosed with one of these problems, your veterinarian can discuss treatment options and prognosis with you.

SAYING GOODBYE

The day will come when you will have to say goodbye to your beloved chinchilla. Your pet may pass on from old age or succumb to a disease or a condition. Your chin may become sickly and might be beyond hope, requiring you to make a decision regarding euthanasia.

Euthanasia is the veterinary process of taking an animal's life. This is done in situations where the animal is in great pain or distress. It is also done in cases where the cost of treating the pet is way beyond the means of the pet's owner.

When veterinarians euthanize a chinchilla, they inject large quantities of a barbiturate into the chin's bloodstream. This drug causes brain function to stop almost immediately, causing the chinchilla to become unconscious. After this happens, the chinchilla stops breathing and the heart stops beating.

In most situations, euthanasia is the kindest, most caring option for a chinchilla that is suffering in pain and has lost his quality of life.

You may opt to have a veterinarian come to your home for the euthanasia process. Doing it this way helps minimize the stress to your already uncomfortable pet. Ask your regular veterinarian if he or she would consider making a house call for you under these circumstances. If not, ask for a referral to a mobile veterinarian. If your vet cannot refer one, look in your telephone directory for a vet that makes house calls. Be sure the vet treats chinchillas. If you can't find a house call vet with experience in chinchilla medicine, ask the vet to consult with your regular veterinarian on the topic of administering euthanasia to your chinchilla.

Many people often wonder if they should be in the room when their pet is euthanized. Some feel compelled to stay by their pet's side to provide comfort. Others are so upset about what is happening that they can't bear the thought of being in the room when the end comes.

The decision about whether to stay with a pet during euthanasia is a very personal one. You should do whatever feels best for you. Do not let anyone pressure you into staying or leaving, or make you feel guilty about your choice. Do what is right for you.

A Final Resting Place

When it comes to disposing of your chin's little body, your

veterinarian can be a good resource. Most veterinary clinics offer cremation options to their clients. You can also contact a local pet cemetery and discuss the various services they provide.

Another option for your chin is burial. If laws in your county permit, you can bury your chin on your property. Or, you can have your pet interred at a local pet cemetery. The cost of reserving a plot for your chin at a pet cemetery may run in the hundreds of dollars. In return, your pet will be placed in a coffin and be given a headstone. Many people prefer to bury their pets at a pet cemetery so they can visit them whenever they wish.

As unpleasant as this is, it's a good idea to think about what you want to do with your chin's remains before your pet passes away. After your pet's death, it will be difficult to make rational decisions. Deciding beforehand eliminates having to deal with this topic while you are grieving.

The Grieving Process

People are often amazed at how devastated they become when they lose a beloved pet. Many folks assume that strong feelings of

With the proper love and care, your chinchilla can be a member of your family for many years. Do all you can to keep your chinchilla happy and healthy.

grief should only be present with the loss of a human being. However, the human heart does not qualify love according to species. For many people, the loss of a pet is as devastating as the loss of a human family member.

Be prepared to feel powerful feelings of loss when you say goodbye to your chinchilla. A variety of emotions will overtake you, including denial, anger, guilt, and depression. Eventually, you will reach a stage of acceptance, and your broken heart will slowly begin to heal.

Unfortunately, those who do not have pets or don't have strong bonds with their animals do not often understand the grief that pet lovers experience when they lose a cherished pet. As a result, grieving pet owners sometimes find themselves alone without anyone to understand or sympathize with the profound grief that has overwhelmed them.

The good news is other devoted pet owners *do* understand what you are feeling, and can provide considerable support in your time of need. After you lose your chinchilla, be careful about who you talk to. Reserve your feelings for other people who are attached to their pets. Odds are they will be sympathetic and give you a shoulder to cry on.

Another option is to contact a pet grief hotline. A number of veterinary schools and other associations provide this service for free to those who have just lost a pet. Pet grief counselors will talk to you about your pet and how you are feeling. Their sympathy can do wonders to help you heal.

The Next Step

It may take a bit of time, or happen soon after you have lost your chinchilla, but eventually, you will probably want to give a home to another one of these delightful pets. While a new chinchilla can never replace the one you have lost, giving a home to another chin can help mend your heart while giving you a new friend to love.

CHINCHILLA Types, Colorations, and Showing

I f you were to take a look at a wild chinchilla and compare it to today's pet chinchillas, you would see a difference in the two animals. Over the decades, domestic chinchillas have changed somewhat in their physical conformation—this is, the way their body parts come together. They have also changed in the way of color.

CHINCHILLA SUBSPECIES

A number of chinchilla subspecies can be found in the wild. Domestic chinchillas are often a blend of three of these different species, and look very different from the wild versions of the subspecies whose natural habitats do not cross over. Because these subspecies do not usually interbreed in the wild because they don't live near each other, domestic chinchillas retain a unique appearance that results from crossing these three types.

All chinchillas have more of one type of chinchilla subspecies in their genes than the others, and so will more closely resemble the wild versions of those subspecies. In the world of chinchilla breeders, these different looks are considered different conformation types.

The three different chinchilla subspecies are the *costina, lanigera,* and the *brevicaulda.* Most chinchillas seen in the pet market today are a blend of *costina* and *lanigera* subspecies.

The *costina* subspecies of chinchillas is the smallest and most slender of the three chinchilla types. Typically weighing less than 20 ounces, *costinas* have a narrow, pointed nose and big, long ears. Their tail is long, and their fur tends to be on the shorter side.

The *lanigera* is bigger than the *costina,* and weighs around 16 to 24 ounces. Its face differs from the *costina* in that it has a straighter, blunter nose. The *lanigera's* tail is longer, and its ears are a bit smaller. The fur of the *lanigera* is thick and long, with a wooly consistency.

The largest of the chinchilla subspecies is the *brevicaulda.* Weighing more than 24 ounces, the *brevicaulda* is rather chunky, and has short, rounder ears and a blunter nose than the other two subspecies. Its tail is shorter than that of the costina and lanigera. The coat of the *brevicaulda* is long and thick and has a wooly feel to it. This subspecies is somewhat rare in the US, and is not often seen in the pet chinchilla market.

Another type of chinchilla is known in Canada, and is called the North American chinchilla. This subspecies is considered a combination of the *costina, lanigera,* and *brevicaulda*, and possesses the best traits of each of these chinchilla types.

CHINCHILLA COLORS

Beyond their physical conformation, domestic chinchillas have changed in an even more dramatic way—in their coloration.

In the mid-1900s, chinchilla breeders in the US started developing what are now called color mutations. These mutations resulted from the births of chinchillas that had colorations different from the bluish-gray coat color most often seen. Instead of culling these chinchillas from the breeding program, breeders began cultivating these unique colorations. In time, the colorations became established within domestic chinchilla populations, and can now be readily found.

The result is that chinchilla lovers now have a variety of colorations to choose from besides the wild, agouti coloration seen on chinchillas before mutations were cultivated. These colorations range from white to black, with a whole lot of colors in between.

The names and descriptions of these different colorations are up for debate among chinchilla breeders, probably because there are so many color possibilities in chinchilla coats. The Empress Chinchilla Breeders Cooperative, the organization that sanctions chinchilla shows throughout the US, re-

There are several different color mutations available to chinchilla hobbyists, including black, white, sapphire, and beige. The chinchilla's coloration has no bearing on its temperament or personality.

cognizes seven mutation chinchilla colorations, in addition to the standard coloration.

Standard

When looking at pet chinchillas, you can expect to see some more common colorations than others. The most commonly seen coloration is the Standard, which is the bluish-gray coat most often associated with chinchillas. This coloration can may be in the agouti pattern—which means the hair shaft of the chinchilla's coat has three or more bands or color—or in a straight, non-agouti pattern. The standard agouti coloration is the color seen in wild chinchillas.

Whites

Under the general category of white chinchillas are a range of light colored coats, including albino (white with red eyes), mosaic (white body patches on a darker color, or dark patches on a white body color), Wilson whites (white with dark eyes), pink white (white with beige veiling) and silvers and stone (light with a silver gray undercoats).

Beiges

The Beige chinchilla comes in any variety of champagne colors, including variations with names like Willman, Tower, and Touch of Velvets. All Beige chinchillas have a white belly.

Ebony/Charcoal

All chinchillas with a blackish coloration on top and a white belly below belong in this category—except for the Black Velvet.

Black Velvet

Chinchillas with this coloration are a stark black coloration with a sharply contrasting white belly.

Sapphire

Only one coloration is found in the Sapphire category: gunmetal blue with a white belly.

Violets

Chinchilla with this coloration resemble a Siamese cat, specifically the blue-point Siamese. The chinchilla has a light body color with a bluish gray area on the face, feet, and tail.

There are several types of white chinchillas. Some have pure white coats and others have silver with light gray undercoats.

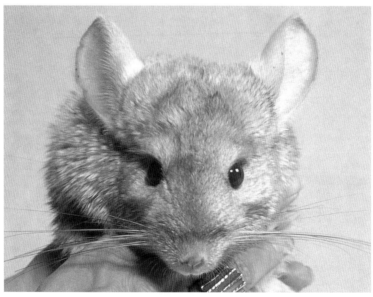

Beige chinchillas have a range of champagne colors. All beige chins have white bellies.

Miscellany

Chinchillas with colorations that do not fit into the above categories are placed in the Miscellany group.

People show horses, dogs, and cats, so why not chinchillas? Chinchilla shows take place around the US and Canada in the spring and fall (when chinchilla coats are at their prime), and are held by groups such as the Empress Chinchilla Breeders Cooperative and the National Canadian Chinchilla Breeders Association.

A Black Velvet chin is black with a white belly. This Black Velvet female is just 18 days old.

No matter what color chinchilla you adopt, you will be getting a loving, devoted pet.

Chinchilla shows can be fascinating to watch. You can learn a lot about chinchillas at such shows, and can meet experts on how to care for these animals. These events also provide rare opportunities to see all the various chinchilla coat mutation colorations in one place. (Be aware that chinchilla pelts are often displayed at shows, which might be upsetting to you or your children.)

If you attend a few chinchilla shows, you may decide you might like to try showing your chin. To do this, you'll need a show-quality chinchilla that you have bred yourself or purchased from a show breeder. You will also need to feed and prepare your pet (show chins require special grooming) so he is able to compete with other high-quality chinchillas.

Contact one of the chinchilla organizations listed in the Resources chapter of this book for more details on how to get involved in showing.

How Shows Work

Chinchilla shows differ from dog, cat, and rabbit shows in that the emphasis is placed on judging animals as a group, rather than individuals. While individual chins win ribbons, more than one first-place winner can be designated if the judge deems that more than one chin deserves the honor. In classes where no chin is deemed worthy of an award, a judge may not give out any ribbons.

Chinchillas are judged in groups of 10 at most US chinchilla shows. Each chinchilla is assigned a cage number, and then judged according to the second numeral in the number pair. For instance, chins in cages 3, 23, 33, and 43 would all be considered part of class 3 and would be judged together.

A chinchilla must be at least four months old to be entered in a show. The classes are divided by colorations, so standards are judged against each other, whites are judged against each other, beiges against each other, etc.

A limit of 20 chinchillas is allowed per entrant in classes held by the Mutation Chinchilla Breeders Association, allowing each entrant to show more than one animal. For example, you could show 20 chins in the Standard class and another 20 total in the Mutation classes. Most pet chinchilla owners don't have these many chinchillas, but many breeders and ranchers enter the most amount of chins in each class that they can.

Coat color is an important factor when judging chinchillas at shows. The judges look for the standard coloration to be a blue-gray with no other hint of color.

Judging Criteria

At chinchilla shows, judges look at various elements in each of the chinchillas they judge. The first criterion is size. Larger chinchillas are preferred, particular when looking at a female chinchilla.

Conformation—that is, the way the animal is put together—is one of the most significant factors in evaluating chinchillas. The type of conformation desired depends on the type of the chinchilla. Generally speaking, chunkier chinchillas are preferred over more lanky specimens.

Coat color is another important factor in judging chinchillas. Judges look for the standard gray coloration to be a bluish gray with no hint of any other color, specifically red, brown, or yellow. Judges look for something they call clarity, which refers to how clear the color is on the coat, and how much blue is present in the chinchilla's fur. The white part of the standard chinchilla should be very white without any gray, brown, or yellow tint. The various mutation colors are also judged according to what is preferred in each of those colorations.

Another important criterion in coat judging is veiling. Veiling is a term that refers to how completely the chinchilla's main coat color covers the animal.

And finally, the density of the chinchilla's coat is of great importance in judging. Judges will exam the chin's coat to determine how plush it is. Chin's with very thick, plush coats are most desired.

When determining which chinchilla will win a given class, the judge weighs all of these criteria together and balances them in his or her mind. The chinchilla that possesses the best quality wins the class.

SHOWING DETAILS

If you decide you want to show chinchillas, you'll need to prepare your pets about two months before the event. Your chinchilla will need to be in top shape before attending the show if he is going to have a chance against the stiff competition.

Start by washing out your chin's cage to get rid of any dirty areas that might stain or harm his coat. Look through the cage for any sharp edges that might do damage to your chinchilla's fur.

Next, let your chinchilla take a dust bath. Once he has finished, give him a water bath. Use lukewarm water with a quality dog or cat shampoo. Wet your chinchilla first, and then lather him up with the

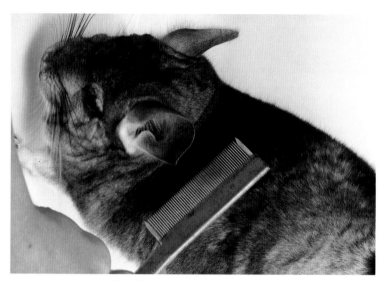

Be sure to groom your chinchilla properly to prepare him for showing. Your chin will need to look his best when he's in a competition.

shampoo, being careful not to get any water or shampoo in his eyes or ears. Thoroughly rinse his coat afterward, being careful to get out all the shampoo. This may take a while since chinchillas have such dense fur.

You can help your chinchilla dry by using a quiet hair dryer with the setting on low. Be careful not to let the air get too hot. You don't want to burn your chinchilla. Once you have taken most of the moisture out of the chin's coat, you can put him back in his cage to finish drying off. Make sure the cage is free from drafts. Twenty-four hours later, let your chin take a dust bath.

Next, you'll need to groom your chin. You can use of any number of tools for this, most of which are available at pet supply stores, through retail catalogs, and on the Internet. A flea comb, stiff brush, or chinchilla comb will do the trick. Brush or comb the fur toward your chinchilla's head, then pick your chinchilla up and quiver your hands to let the fur settle back to its usual place. If static cling develops in your chin's coat, go over the coat with a lint remover to make the static disappear.

Meanwhile, your chin's diet will need to be adjusted to get him into showing condition. Add cracked corn, flax seed, wheat germ, or sunflower seeds to his diet in small amounts over a gradual period of time. These foods will help bring the best out of his coat. Make sure he has access to plenty of fresh hay.

Let your chinchilla take a dust bath every day to keep his coat in good condition. Brush or comb his coat every few days up until a week before the show to keep it looking good.

A week before the event, it's time to do some last minute cleaning up. Examine your chinchilla to see if his coat is stained, or his white parts are beginning to yellow. In either case, you can add half a cup of cornstarch to his dust bath, along with two cups of white cornmeal. These additives will help bring out the whiteness in his coat.

The week before the show, have your chin take a dust bath each day. Groom the fur in the middle of the week, and then again the day before the show.

Going to the Show

You may need to stay overnight in a hotel the day before the chinchilla show. If this is the case, find out from the chin club which hotel is closest to the venue and allows pets. Be sure to book your hotel room early, since the hotel may fill up quickly once the show is announced.

Take your chinchilla to the show in a crate meant for transporting small animals. If you will be spending the night at a hotel, be sure to bring a separate chinchilla cage for your pet to sleep in. Don't forget his regular food, bedding, and water bottle.

If you are only taking your chin to the show for the day, just bring his water bottle and some hay. Be aware that if water spills on your chin on the day of the show, it may ruin his coat for that day's judging. It's a good idea to offer your chin some water early in the day, and every couple of hours, rather than leaving the bottle in his cage at all times.

When you are handling your chinchilla at the show, try to avoid holding him by the body as much as possible. The fur can come loose with handling, and when you present your pet to the judge, the coat may be unacceptable.

For more information about the details of entering a show, registering your chinchilla, and finding a show near you, contact a chinchilla club or organizations.

GLOSSARY

Agouti—The color pattern seen in wild chinchillas.

Antibiotics—Medications used to treat bacterial infections.

Bathhouse—A small plastic structure in the shape of a house that can be filled with chinchilla dust for bathing purposes.

Breeder—Person who keeps animals for reproduction purposes and sells the offspring, either for pets or for pelts.

Chinchilla dust—A mixture of sand and dust (often volcanic) that is used by chinchillas to keep their coats healthy.

Chinchilla harness—A harness made specifically to restrain chinchillas.

Convention on International Trade of Endangered Animals (CITES)—Agreement made between South America and a number of other countries to limit the trade and export of endangered species and products produced among them.

Den—A small enclosure where chinchillas hide and raise their young.

Exercise wheel— A wheel with a broad, flat edge that allows the chinchilla to run inside.

Exotics veterinarian—A veterinary doctor who specializes in treating rodents, reptiles, birds, and other unusual pets.

Hay cubes—A small, four-sided cube of compressed hay.

Hide box—A human-made version of a den, usually constructed from wood.

Incisors—The four front teeth of a rodent (two upper and two lower).

Malocclusion—A condition where the incisors are not properly aligned, and so do not wear down properly during the course of the chinchilla's life.

Molars—The back teeth.

Mutation— A change from the standard coat color, resulting from a recessive gene.

Neuter—Castration of the male chinchilla.

Nocturnal—The behavior of sleeping during the day and being active at night.

Pedigree—A listing of a show chinchilla's parentage.

Pellets—Commercially prepared food, available in bags or boxes.

Rancher—One who breeds chinchillas for fur.

Rescue group—Group of individuals who place unwanted chinchillas in new homes.

Spay—Removal of the female reproduction system.

Standard coloration—The grayish-blue coloration most often seen in chinchillas.

Veiling—reference to how completely the chinchilla's main coat color covers the animal.

RESOURCES

ORGANIZATIONS

California Chins
333 Marmona Drive
Menlo Park, CA 94025
E-mail: chinmom@sbcglobal.net
www.cachins.org

The Chinchilla Club
(The International Pet Chinchilla Organization)
E-mail: info@chinclub.net
www.chinclub.net

National Chinchilla Breeders of Canada
RR#2 Norval
Ontario, Canada
L0P 1K0
E-mail: ncbc@idirect.com
www.chinnet.com/misc/ncbc.html

National Chinchilla Society (UK)
Phone: 01457 856945
E-mail: natchinsoc@freeuk.com
www.natchinsoc.freeuk.com

RESCUE AND ADOPTION ORGANIZATIONS

The American Society for the Prevention of Cruelty to Animals
424 East 92nd Street
New York, NY 10128-6801
(212) 876-7700
www.aspca.org
E-mail: information@aspca.org

The Humane Society of the United States (HSUS)
2100 L Street, NW
Washington, DC 20037
Phone: (202)- 452-1100
www.hsus.org

PUBLICATIONS

Critters USA
Fancy Publications, Inc.
3 Burroughs
Irvine, CA 92618
Phone: (888) 738-2665
Fax: (949) 855-3045
E-mail: critters@fancypubs.com
www.fancypubs.com

INTERNET RESOURCES

The Chinchilla Club
www.chinclub.net
This website of the international club for chinchilla owners provides breeder and veterinarian directories, event and news announcements, and gives information on care, shopping, and feeding.

Chin Net
www.chinnet.net
This website provides information on housing, feeding, where to buy your chinchilla, and even genetics. You can also chat with other chinchilla owners online.

Etc. Chinchilla Page
www.etc-etc.com/chin.htm
The Etc. Chinchilla website features articles, pictures, and chinchilla website links, as well as information on the history of chinchillas as pets.

Pet Net's Chinchilla Online Pet Reference
www.pet-net.net/small_animals/chinchillas.htm
This website provides detailed information on breeders, chinchilla rescue, products, and books on chinchilla care.

EMERGENCY SERVICES

ASPCA National Animal Poison Control Center
1-888-426-4435
www.aspca.org

Animal Poison Hotline
(888) 232-8870

VETERINARY RESOURCES

The American Veterinary Medical Association
1931 North Meacham Road, Suite 100
Schaumburg, IL 60173
Phone: (847) 925-8070
Fax: (847) 925-1329
E-mail: avmainfo@avma.org
www.avma.org

INDEX

PHOTO CREDITS